5A

W9-BES-193

# PRIMARY MATHEMATICS Standards Edition

## WORKBOOK

**Marshall Cavendish** Education

Original edition published under the title Primary Mathematics Workbook 5A
© 1983 Curriculum Planning & Development Division, Ministry of Education, Singapore
Published by Times Media Private Limited

This edition © 2008 Marshall Cavendish International (Singapore) Private Limited
© 2014 Marshall Cavendish Education Pte Ltd

**Published by Marshall Cavendish Education**
Times Centre, 1 New Industrial Road, Singapore 536196
Customer Service Hotline: (65) 6213 9688
US Office Tel: (1-914) 332 8888 | Fax: (1-914) 332 8882
E-mail: cs@mceducation.com
Website: www.mceducation.com

Marshall Cavendish Corporation
99 White Plains Road
Tarrytown, NY 10591
U.S.A.
Tel: (1-914) 332 8888
Fax: (1-914) 332 8882
E-mail: mcc@marshallcavendish.com
Website: www.marshallcavendish.com

First published 2008
Reprinted 2009 (twice), 2010 (twice), 2011 (twice), 2012 (twice), 2013, 2014, 2015 (twice), 2016, 2017, 2018 (fourth)
            2019, 2020 (fourth)

All rights reserved.

No part of this publication may be reproduced, stored in a retrieval system or transmitted,
in any form or by any means, electronic, mechanical, photocopying, recording or otherwise,
without the prior permission of the copyright owner. Any requests for permission should be
addressed to the Publisher.

Marshall Cavendish is a registered trademark of Times Publishing Limited.

Singapore Math® is a trademark of Singapore Math Inc.® and
Marshall Cavendish Education Pte Ltd.

Primary Mathematics (Standards Edition) Workbook 5A
ISBN 978-0-7614-6999-5

Printed in Singapore

Primary Mathematics (Standards Edition) is adapted from Primary Mathematics Workbook 5A (3rd Edition), originally
developed by the Ministry of Education, Singapore. This edition contains new content developed by Marshall Cavendish
International (Singapore) Private Limited, which is not attributable to the Ministry of Education, Singapore.

We would like to acknowledge the Project Team from the Ministry of Education, Singapore, that developed the original
Singapore Edition:
Project Director: Dr Kho Tek Hong
Team Members: Hector Chee Kum Hoong, Liang Hin Hoon, Lim Eng Tann,
            Rosalind Lim Hui Cheng, Ng Hwee Wan, Ng Siew Lee
Curriculum Specialists: Christina Cheong Ngan Peng, Ho Juan Beng, Sin Kwai Meng

Our thanks to Richard Askey, Emeritus Professor of Mathematics (University of Wisconsin, Madison) and Madge Goldman,
President (Gabriella and Paul Rosenbaum Foundation), for their help and advice in the production of Primary Mathematics
(Standards Edition).

We would also like to recognize the contributions of Jennifer Kempe (Curriculum Advisor, Singapore Math Inc.®) and
Bill Jackson (Math Coach, School No. 2, Paterson, New Jersey) to Primary Mathematics (Standards Edition).

# CONTENTS

**1  Whole Numbers**

| | | |
|---|---|---:|
| Exercise | 1 | 5 |
| Exercise | 2 | 7 |
| Exercise | 3 | 9 |
| Exercise | 4 | 12 |
| Exercise | 5 | 14 |
| Exercise | 6 | 16 |
| Exercise | 7 | 18 |
| **REVIEW** | **1** | **20** |

**2  More Calculations with Whole Numbers**

| | | |
|---|---|---:|
| Exercise | 1 | 22 |
| Exercise | 2 | 24 |
| Exercise | 3 | 25 |
| Exercise | 4 | 27 |
| Exercise | 5 | 29 |
| Exercise | 6 | 32 |
| Exercise | 7 | 35 |
| Exercise | 8 | 37 |
| Exercise | 9 | 38 |
| Exercise | 10 | 39 |
| Exercise | 11 | 40 |
| **REVIEW** | **2** | **41** |

**3  Fractions**

| | | |
|---|---|---:|
| Exercise | 1 | 46 |
| Exercise | 2 | 50 |
| Exercise | 3 | 52 |
| Exercise | 4 | 54 |
| Exercise | 5 | 56 |
| Exercise | 6 | 58 |
| Exercise | 7 | 60 |
| Exercise | 8 | 62 |
| Exercise | 9 | 64 |
| Exercise | 10 | 66 |

| | | | |
|---|---|---|--:|
| | Exercise | 11 | 68 |
| | Exercise | 12 | 70 |
| | Exercise | 13 | 72 |
| | Exercise | 14 | 74 |
| | **REVIEW** | **3** | **76** |

**4   Multiply and Divide Fractions**

| | | | |
|---|---|---|--:|
| | Exercise | 1 | 79 |
| | Exercise | 2 | 81 |
| | Exercise | 3 | 83 |
| | Exercise | 4 | 85 |
| | Exercise | 5 | 87 |
| | Exercise | 6 | 89 |
| | Exercise | 7 | 91 |
| | Exercise | 8 | 93 |
| | Exercise | 9 | 94 |
| | Exercise | 10 | 95 |
| | Exercise | 11 | 96 |
| | Exercise | 12 | 98 |
| | **REVIEW** | **4** | **102** |

**5   Perimeter, Area and Surface Area**

| | | | |
|---|---|---|--:|
| | Exercise | 1 | 106 |
| | Exercise | 2 | 108 |
| | Exercise | 3 | 109 |
| | Exercise | 4 | 113 |
| | Exercise | 5 | 116 |
| | Exercise | 6 | 119 |
| | Exercise | 7 | 121 |
| | **REVIEW** | **5** | **123** |

**6   Ratio**

| | | | |
|---|---|---|--:|
| | Exercise | 1 | 129 |
| | Exercise | 2 | 131 |
| | Exercise | 3 | 133 |
| | Exercise | 4 | 135 |
| | Exercise | 5 | 137 |
| | **REVIEW** | **6** | **138** |

# EXERCISE 1

1.  Write the numbers in words.
    (a) 104,102

    [                                    ]

    (b) 65,598,000

    [                                    ]

    (c) 11,011,011,011

    [                                    ]

2.  Write in standard form.
    (a) nine billion, nine million, nine hundred thousand, nine [        ]

    (b) fifteen million, fifteen [        ]

    (c) one million, one thousand, one [        ]

3.  Check (✔) the box beside each true statement.
    (a) Three thousand more than 54,013,020 is 54,043,020. [   ]

    (b) Twenty million more than 5,871,800,025 is 5,891,800,025. [   ]

    (c) Fifty thousand less than 10,000,000 is 9,950,000. [   ]

    (d) One hundred thousand less than 123,456,789 is 122,456,789. [   ]

    (e) Five million less than 255,000,000 is 205,000,000. [   ]

4.  Fill in the blanks.
    (a) $6,000,000 + 50,000 + 4000 + 10 =$ [        ]

    (b) $35,200,000,000 + 3,000,000 + 800,000 + 500 =$ [        ]

(c) $7{,}000{,}000 + $ ☐ $ + 2000 + 5 = 7{,}852{,}005$

(d) $36{,}000{,}000{,}000 + $ ☐ $ + 700{,}000 + 50{,}000$
    $= 37{,}000{,}750{,}000$

5. Write > or < in each ◯.

(a) $9{,}999{,}999{,}999$ ◯ $10{,}000{,}000{,}000$

(b) $32{,}586{,}153$ ◯ $8{,}985{,}653$

(c) $54{,}013{,}020$ ◯ forty million, nine hundred thousand, twenty-two

(d) $358{,}568{,}486$ ◯ One billion

# EXERCISE 2

1. Round each number to the nearest ten thousand.
   (a) 10,600

   (b) 234,200

   (c) 459,900

2. Round each number to the nearest hundred thousand.
   (a) 1,585,100

   (b) 15,851,000

   (c) 158,510,000

3. Round each number to the nearest million.
   (a) 8,385,000

   (b) 35,680,800

   (c) 555,555,555

4. Round each number to the nearest ten million.
   (a) 287,185,000

   (b) 652,100,600

   (c) 69,103,301

5. Round each number to the nearest hundred million.

   (a) 180,169,400 _____

   (b) 7,658,588,102 _____

   (c) 51,609,560,005 _____

6. The population of California in 2005 was 36,132,147. Approximately how many hundred thousand people is this? _____

7. The maximum distance of Mars from the sun is about 155 million miles. Which of the following numbers could this be an approximation for?

   15,468,000   155,568,000   154,658,000   155,034,000 _____

# EXERCISE 3

1.  Add.

    | | |
    |---|---|
    | (a) | 2,700,000 + 900,000 = |
    | (b) | 800,000 + 500,000 = |
    | (c) | 3,200,000 + 800,000 = |

2.  Subtract.

    | | |
    |---|---|
    | (a) | 5,300,000 − 400,000 = |
    | (b) | 600,000 − 200,000 = |
    | (c) | 4,500,000 − 600,000 = |

3.  Multiply.

    | | |
    |---|---|
    | (a) | 80,000 × 2 = |
    | (b) | 50,000 × 4 = |
    | (c) | 200,000 × 6 = |

4.  Divide.

    | | |
    |---|---|
    | (a) | 180,000 ÷ 6 = |
    | (b) | 240,000 ÷ 8 = |
    | (c) | 560,000 ÷ 7 = |

5. Estimate the value of each of the following.

| |
|---|
| (a) 306,481 + 560,423 ≈ 300,000 + 600,000 <br> = |
| (b) 483,176 + 820,533 ≈ |
| (c) 2,546,831 + 692,500 ≈ |
| (d) 8,672,390 + 920,767 ≈ |
| (e) 735,601 − 398,842 ≈ |
| (f) 930,652 − 456,841 ≈ |
| (g) 3,654,704 − 886,512 ≈ |
| (h) 6,300,649 − 100,874 ≈ |

6. Estimate the value of each of the following.

(a) 330,667 × 2 ≈ 300,000 × 2
   =

330,667 ≈ 300,000

(b) 481,192 × 4 ≈

(c) 828,676 × 6 ≈

(d) 956,057 × 5 ≈

(e) 614,689 ÷ 3 ≈ 600,000 ÷ 3
   =

(f) 475,999 ÷ 6 ≈

(g) 526,843 ÷ 5 ≈

(h) 639,813 ÷ 9 ≈

# EXERCISE 4

1. Find the factors of each of the following numbers.

(a) 48

$48 = 1 \times 48$   $48 = 3 \times 16$   $48 = 6 \times 8$

$48 = 2 \times 24$   $48 = 4 \times 12$

The factors of 48 are _____.

(b) 72

(c) 128

(d) 150

2. What number am I?

(a) I am between 20 and 40.
    I am a multiple of 5.
    I am a factor of 60.

    I am _____.

(b) I am smaller than 80.
    I am a common multiple of 8 and 10.

    I am _____.

(c) I am bigger than 10.
    I am a common multiple of 24 and 36.

    I am _____.

(d) I am a common multiple of 2, 4 and 7.

    I am _____.

# EXERCISE 5

1. List all the prime numbers between 1 and 50. Use the number chart below to help you.

| 1 | 2 | 3 | 4 | 5 | 6 | 7 | 8 | 9 | 10 |
|---|---|---|---|---|---|---|---|---|----|
| 11 | 12 | 13 | 14 | 15 | 16 | 17 | 18 | 19 | 20 |
| 21 | 22 | 23 | 24 | 25 | 26 | 27 | 28 | 29 | 30 |
| 31 | 32 | 33 | 34 | 35 | 36 | 37 | 38 | 39 | 40 |
| 41 | 42 | 43 | 44 | 45 | 46 | 47 | 48 | 49 | 50 |

2. List the prime numbers between 50 and 60.

3. Fill in the blanks with prime numbers.

   (a) $5 \times 4 = 5 \times$ ☐ $\times$ ☐

   (b) $6 \times 9 =$ ☐ $\times 3 \times 3 \times 3$

   (c) $45 \times 2 =$ ☐ $\times$ ☐ $\times 3 \times 2$

   (d) $14 \times 6 = 2 \times$ ☐ $\times 2 \times$ ☐

4. Write >, < or = in each ◯.

   (a) $3^4$ ◯ $3 \times 4$

   (b) $2^2$ ◯ $2 \times 2$

   (c) $2^3$ ◯ $2 \times 2 \times 2$

   (d) $4^3$ ◯ $3 \times 3 \times 3 \times 3$

   (e) $5 \times 5 \times 5$ ◯ $3^5$

   (f) $7^4$ ◯ $49 \times 49$

   (g) $36$ ◯ $62$

   (h) $3^2 \times 2^3$ ◯ $9 \times 8$

5. Rewrite the following prime factorizations using exponents.

(a) $2 \times 2 \times 3 \times 5$

$\boxed{\phantom{xxxxxx}}$

(b) $7 \times 11 \times 7 \times 11 \times 2$

$\boxed{\phantom{xxxxxx}}$

(c) $3 \times 2 \times 3 \times 2 \times 3$

$\boxed{\phantom{xxxxxx}}$

(d) $7 \times 7 \times 3 \times 3 \times 2$

$\boxed{\phantom{xxxxxx}}$

6. List the composite numbers between 47 and 51 and show the prime factorization of each.

# EXERCISE 6

1. Multiply.

| | |
|---|---|
| (a) 254 × 10 = | (b) 602 × 100 = |
| (c) 93 × 40 = | (d) 57 × 1000 = |
| (e) 43 × 600 = | (f) 392 × 800 = |
| (g) 728 × 5000 = | (h) 8056 × 3000 = |

2. Estimate the value of each of the following.

(a) $326 \times 47 \approx 300 \times 50$

$\quad = $

(b) $78 \times 586 \approx$

(c) $32 \times 705 \approx$

(d) $4165 \times 53 \approx$

3. Andrew wants to buy 28 radio sets. Each radio set costs $229. Give a quick estimate of the total cost of the radio sets.

4. Give a quick estimate of the area of a rectangle with length 114 in. and width 92 in.

# EXERCISE 7

1. Divide.

| | |
|---|---|
| (a) 360 ÷ 10 = | (b) 4200 ÷ 100 = |
| (c) 250 ÷ 50 = | (d) 5600 ÷ 800 = |
| (e) 1050 ÷ 70 = | (f) 60,000 ÷ 400 = |
| (g) 630,000 ÷ 9000 = | (h) 960,000 ÷ 6000 = |

2. Estimate the value of each of the following.

(a) $282 \div 52 \approx 300 \div 50$
$$=$$

(b) $324 \div 42 \approx$

(c) $4406 \div 49 \approx$

(d) $1705 \div 31 \approx$

3. Albert bought 28 compact discs for $805. Give a quick estimate of the cost of each compact disc.

4. The floor area of a hall is 1044 m². The length is 36 m. Give a quick estimate of the width of the hall.

# REVIEW 1

1. Write 3,495,002,091 in expanded form.

   [                                                    ]

2. Write in standard form.

   (a) 60 millions                               [        ]

   (b) 5 billions 605 thousands                  [        ]

   (c) 7 millions 80 hundreds                    [        ]

   (d) 4 billions 2 millions 3 thousands         [        ]

3. Write >, < or = in each ◯.

   (a) 13,268,000 ◯ 31,862,000

   (b) 13,249,650, ◯ 13,242,650

   (c) 33,856,000 − 1,000,000 ◯ 30,856,000

   (d) 657,300 + 10,000 ◯ 667,300

   (e) 37,000 + 8,000 ◯ 50,000 − 4,000

   (f) 80000 x 3 ◯ 60 × 400

   (g) 400 × 50 ◯ 10,000,000 ÷ 500

4. Estimate the value of

   (a) 6903 × 22          [        ]

   (b) 8548 × 329         [        ]

   (c) 9869 × 899         [        ]

(d) 37,496 ÷ 603 ☐

(e) 55,349 ÷ 7168 ☐

(f) 71,375 ÷ 8236 ☐

5. Find the common factors of 18 and 24. ☐

6. Find the first two common multiples of 8 and 12. ☐

7. Express the following using exponents.
   (a) 3 × 3 × 2 × 2 × 5 ☐

   (b) 11 × 7 × 13 × 7 × 11 ☐

8. Express the following as a product of prime factors using exponents.
   (a) 74

   (b) 60

   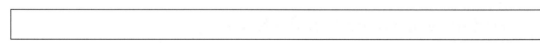

## EXERCISE 1

1. Fill in the blanks.

   (a) 60 + 21 + 40 + 19 = ⬚

   (b) 18 + 27 + 22 + 10 = ⬚

   (c) 25 × 18 × 4 = ⬚

   (d) 150 × 7 × 5 × 2 = ⬚

2. Check (✔) the box beside each true statement.

   (a) 8 + 9 + 12 + 10 = 10 + 12 + 9 + 8 ⬚

   (b) 6 × 9 × 11 = 9 × 11 × 6 ⬚

   (c) 9 × 5 + 3 = 9 + 5 × 3 ⬚

   (d) 6 + 8 + 2 × 10 = 6 + 8 × 10 + 2 ⬚

   Find the value of each of the following.

3. (a) 138 + (20 − 15) ⬚

   (b) 138 + 20 − 15 ⬚

   (c) 138 − 20 + 15 ⬚

   (d) (138 − 20) + 15 ⬚

   (e) (64 ÷ 8) ÷ 2 ⬚

   (f) 64 ÷ (8 ÷ 2) ⬚

   (g) 64 ÷ 8 ÷ 2 ⬚

   (h) 99 ÷ 3 × 3 ⬚

   (i) (99 ÷ 3) × 3 ⬚

4. (a) $7 \times 9 + 1 \div 1 - 6 \times 3$

   (b) $(108 + 12) \div 5 \times 6$

   (c) $60 \div 5 + 24$

   (d) $20 - 36 \div 6 + 4$

   (e) $49 \div 7 \div 7$

   (f) $(20 - 16) \times (9 - 2)$

   (g) $56 - 8 \times 6$

   (h) $45 - 9 \div 3$

   (i) $300 \div (8 + 2) \times 10$

# EXERCISE 2

1. Check (✔) the box beside each true statement.

   (a) $(8 - 3) \times 5 = (8 \times 5) - (3 \times 5)$ ☐

   (b) $(8 - 3) \times 5 = (8 \times 3) - (5 \times 3)$ ☐

   (c) $(7 + 6) \times 9 = (7 + 9) \times (6 + 9)$ ☐

   (d) $(7 + 6) \times 9 = (7 \times 9) + (6 \times 9)$ ☐

2. Fill in the missing numbers.

   (a) $(77 + 6) \times 7 = (77 \times \boxed{\phantom{xxxx}}) + (6 \times \boxed{\phantom{xxxx}})$

   (b) $(15 + 9) \times 9 = (15 \times \boxed{\phantom{xxxx}}) + (9 \times \boxed{\phantom{xxxx}})$

   (c) $6 \times (21 - 16) = (6 \times \boxed{\phantom{xxxx}}) - (6 \times \boxed{\phantom{xxxx}})$

   (d) $9 \times (12 - 7) = (9 \times 12) - (9 \times \boxed{\phantom{xxxx}})$

   (e) $(8 \times 5) + (8 \times 4) = 8 \times (5 + \boxed{\phantom{xxxx}})$

   (f) $(28 - 3) \times 7 = (\boxed{\phantom{xxxx}} \times 7) - (3 \times \boxed{\phantom{xxxx}})$

   (g) $(2 \times 9) + (10 \times 9) = (\boxed{\phantom{xxxx}} + \boxed{\phantom{xxxx}}) \times 9$

3. (a) $26 \times 11 = (27 \times \boxed{\phantom{xxxx}}) - (1 \times \boxed{\phantom{xxxx}})$

   (b) $55 \times 10 = (56 \times 10) - (\boxed{\phantom{xxxx}} \times 10)$

   (c) $98 \times 7 = (97 \times 7) + (\boxed{\phantom{xxxx}} \times 7)$

   (d) $63 \times 5 = (\boxed{\phantom{xxxx}} \times 5) + (1 \times 5)$

# EXERCISE 3

1. Add.

(a) 399 + 54 =

399 + 54 = 400 + 54 − 1

(b) 1467 + 299 =

(c) 201 + 679 =

1 + 79

(d) 2043 + 207 =

(e) 520 + 380 =

20 + 80

(f) 2432 + 368 =

(g) 1563 + 437 =

563 + 437

(h) 3254 + 746 =

2. Subtract.

(a) 312 − 99 =

312 − 99 = 312 − 100 + 1

(b) 4825 − 399 =

(c) 700 − 87 =

100 − 87

(d) 1200 − 45 =

(e) 3600 − 589 =

600 − 589

(f) 5460 − 56 =

(g) 4000 − 786 =

1000 − 786

(h) 5000 − 85 =

# EXERCISE 4

1.  Multiply.

(a) 52 × 41 =

52 × 41 = 52 × 40 + 52

(b) 46 × 51 =

(c) 75 × 21 =

(d) 28 × 81 =

(e) 62 × 99 =

62 × 99 = 62 × 100 − 62

(f) 34 × 99 =

(g) 99 × 65 =

(h) 99 × 47 =

2. Multiply.

(a) $26 \times 49 =$

$26 \times 49 = 26 \times 50 - 26$

(b) $88 \times 29 =$

(c) $59 \times 36 =$

(d) $79 \times 54 =$

(e) $25 \times 32 =$

$25 \times 32 = 25 \times 4 \times 8$

(f) $25 \times 80 =$

(g) $56 \times 25 =$

(h) $88 \times 25 =$

# EXERCISE 5

Find the missing numbers.

1.

(a) 2482 + _____ = 3417

(b) _____ + 783 = 6004

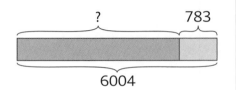

(c) 1058 − _____ = 469

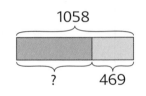

(d) _____ − 472 = 2983

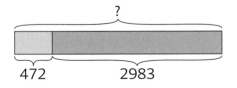

Find the missing numbers.

2. | (a) 4 × _____ = 616

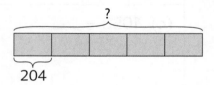

(b) _____ × 7 = 1435

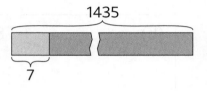

(c) _____ ÷ 5 = 204

(d) 333 ÷ _____ = 9

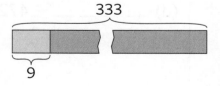

3. At a carnival, Ann sold 314 bottles of drinks a day. She sold 66 bottles more in the afternoon than in the morning. How many bottles of drinks did she sell in the morning?

_____

4. Adam bought a pen. He also bought a book which cost 3 times as much as the pen. He spent $112 altogether. Find the cost of the book.

# EXERCISE 6

1.  Elaine has 274 beads. 150 of them are blue, 70 are red and the rest
    are white. How many more red beads than white beads are there?

2.  Tickets to a concert cost $15 per adult and $8 per child. Matthew
    bought tickets for 4 adults and 5 children. How much did he spend
    altogether?

3. Chris paid $36 for 3 similar tank-tops and 2 similar T-shirts. A T-shirt cost 3 times as much as a tank-top. How much did Chris pay for the 2 T-shirts?

4. Peter bought 45 greeting cards at 3 for $2. He sold all of them at 5 for $4. How much money did he earn?

5. A box of cookies cost $6 and a bottle of milk cost $2. After paying for 2 boxes of cookies and 6 bottles of milk, Nicole had $30 left. How much money did she have at first?

6. Lily and Sara each had an equal amount of money at first. After Lily spent $18 and Sara spent $25, Lily had twice as much as Sara. How much money did each of them have at first?

# EXERCISE 7

Multiply.

1.

| | |
|---|---|
| (a) 78 × 40 = <br><br> $\begin{array}{r} 78 \\ \times\ 40 \\ \hline \end{array}$ | (b) 46 × 50 = |
| (c) 53 × 24 = | (d) 65 × 89 = |
| (e) 246 × 70 = | (f) 309 × 60 = |
| (g) 508 × 32 = | (h) 760 × 87 = |

2.

(a) 1257 × 30 =

$$\begin{array}{r} 1257 \\ \times \quad 30 \\ \hline \end{array}$$

(b) 4008 × 70 =

(c) 1870 × 20 =

(d) 6229 × 13 =

(e) 3424 × 25 =

(f) 1003 × 63 =

(g) 1075 × 73 =

(h) 8207 × 46 =

# EXERCISE 8

1.  Divide.

| | |
|---|---|
| (a)  $60 \div 20 =$<br><br>$20 \overline{)60}$ | (b)  $94 \div 30 =$ |
| (c)  $790 \div 80 =$ | (d)  $577 \div 90 =$ |
| (e)  $98 \div 32 =$ | (f)  $88 \div 49 =$ |
| (g)  $580 \div 64 =$ | (h)  $299 \div 53 =$ |

# EXERCISE 9

1. Divide.

| | |
|---|---|
| (a) $92 \div 17 =$ <br><br> $17\overline{)92}$ | (b) $85 \div 22 =$ |
| (c) $80 \div 26 =$ | (d) $96 \div 34 =$ |
| (e) $361 \div 62 =$ | (f) $397 \div 47 =$ |
| (g) $425 \div 54 =$ | (h) $192 \div 38 =$ |

# EXERCISE 10

1. Divide.

| | |
|---|---|
| (a) $528 \div 30 =$ <br><br> $30\overline{)528}$ | (b) $820 \div 40 =$ |
| (c) $307 \div 20 =$ | (d) $650 \div 50 =$ |
| (e) $485 \div 15 =$ | (f) $700 \div 21 =$ |
| (g) $820 \div 42 =$ | (h) $908 \div 56 =$ |

# EXERCISE 11

1. Divide.

| | |
|---|---|
| (a) $9963 \div 41 =$  <br><br> $41\overline{)9963}$ | (b) $8282 \div 16 =$ |
| (c) $6600 \div 55 =$ | (d) $9229 \div 29 =$ |
| (e) $2624 \div 32 =$ | (f) $5821 \div 63 =$ |
| (g) $7801 \div 48 =$ | (h) $3008 \div 25 =$ |

# REVIEW 2

1. Write the following in words.

   (a) 2,044,000

   [                    ]

   (b) 15,508,000

   [                    ]

   (c) 376,920,000

   [                    ]

   (d) 6,400,000,000

   [                    ]

2. Write the following in figures.

   (a) four thousand, eight                              [        ]

   (b) twenty-seven thousand, three hundred             [        ]

   (c) sixty billion, eleven                             [        ]

   (d) twelve million, nine hundred four thousand       [        ]

3. Find the value of each of the following.

   (a) 500,000 + 80,000 + 300                           [        ]

   (b) 60,000,000 + 420,000 + 5000                      [        ]

4. (a) In 8,453,000, the digit [        ] is in the hundred thousands place.

   (b) In 5,236,000, the digit 3 stands for 3 × [        ].

5.  (a) 8,206,000 is 1,000,000 more than ☐.

    (b) 62,440,000 is 1,000,000 less than ☐.

    (c) 9,345,000 is ☐ more than 9,305,000.

    (d) 7,188,000 is ☐ less than 7,988,000.

6.  (a) Which is greater, 45,832 or 45,382? ☐

    (b) Which is smaller, 30,012 or 30,102? ☐

7.  Arrange the following numbers in decreasing order.
    64,748, 76,435, 87,660, 60,083
    ☐

8.  (a) List all the factors of 24.
    ☐

    (b) Write the first twelve multiples of 6.
    ☐

9.  Which one of the following is the smallest?
    90,786, 84,007, 91,000, 80,999 ☐

10. Find the value of each of the following.
    (a) 130 + 50 + 20 + 70 + 50 ☐

    (b) 145 − 25 × 4 ☐

    (c) 228 ÷ 6 × 2 ☐

(d) $306 - 45 \div 9$      ▢

(e) $440 - 64 + 36 \div 6$      ▢

(f) $8 - 20 \div (5 \times 4)$      ▢

(g) $8 - 16 \div 4 + 1 \times 2$      ▢

(h) $41 - 21 \div 7 + 3 \times 9$      ▢

(i) $3 \times 6 - 12 + 10 \div 5$      ▢

(j) $4 - 7 \div (4 + 3) \times 3$      ▢

(k) $3^4 \times 5^2$      ▢

11. Write the prime factorization of 200.

▢

12. (a) Round 49,501 to the nearest hundred.      ▢

(b) Round 49,501 to the nearest thousand.      ▢

13. (a) Find the sum of 12,099 and 900.      ▢

(b) Find the difference between 79 and 2100.      ▢

(c) Find the product of 540 and 28.      ▢

(d) Find the quotient and remainder when 127 is divided by 40.      ▢

14. 200 children took part in a concert. There were 4 times as many girls as boys.

(a) How many girls were there?      ▢

(b) How many more girls than boys were there?      ▢

15. Miguel had 45 melons. He sold 25 of them at $6 each and sold the rest at $4 each. How much money did he receive?

---

16. Ashley bought a bed for $295. She also bought 2 mattresses at $65 each. She gave the cashier a $500 note. How much change did she receive?

17. Brandy has 278 stamps. Jane has 64 stamps more than Brandy. Sam and Jane have 500 stamps altogether. How many stamps does Sam have?

---

18. Mrs. Peters baked 156 fruit pies for a fruit fair. She sold them in boxes containing 12 fruit pies each. Each box cost $18. How much money did she collect?

# EXERCISE 1

1. Find the missing number in each of the following.

(a) $\dfrac{4}{5} = \dfrac{12}{\square}$

(b) $\dfrac{3}{7} = \dfrac{\square}{28}$

(c) $\dfrac{25}{\square} = \dfrac{5}{8}$

(d) $\dfrac{6}{9} = \dfrac{2}{\square}$

(e) $\dfrac{2}{12} = \dfrac{\square}{6}$

(f) $\dfrac{5}{\square} = \dfrac{10}{12}$

2.  Express each of the following as an improper fraction.

| | |
|---|---|
| (a) $1\frac{2}{3}$ | (b) $1\frac{5}{7}$ |
| (c) $2\frac{1}{4}$ | (d) $2\frac{3}{8}$ |
| (e) $3\frac{1}{6}$ | (f) $2\frac{4}{9}$ |
| (g) $2\frac{9}{10}$ | (h) $3\frac{5}{12}$ |

3. Express each of the following as a whole number or a mixed number in its simplest form.

| | |
|---|---|
| (a) $\frac{14}{3}$ | (b) $\frac{22}{4}$ |
| (c) $\frac{15}{6}$ | (d) $\frac{30}{5}$ |
| (e) $\frac{21}{7}$ | (f) $\frac{20}{8}$ |
| (g) $\frac{17}{10}$ | (h) $\frac{26}{12}$ |

4. Write **>**, **<** or **=** in each ◯.

(a) $1\frac{1}{12}$ ◯ $1\frac{9}{10}$

(b) $2\frac{3}{10}$ ◯ $2\frac{1}{2}$

(c) $\frac{27}{9}$ ◯ $3$

(d) $2$ ◯ $1\frac{11}{12}$

(e) $3\frac{4}{5}$ ◯ $\frac{38}{10}$

(f) $\frac{25}{8}$ ◯ $3\frac{1}{9}$

5. (a) Arrange these numbers in increasing order.

$\frac{13}{3}$, $3\frac{3}{9}$, $4$, $3\frac{1}{2}$, $\frac{9}{2}$

(b) Arrange these numbers in decreasing order.

$3\frac{1}{12}$, $5\frac{1}{3}$, $6$, $\frac{15}{3}$, $4\frac{9}{10}$

# EXERCISE 2

1.  Write each of the following as an improper fraction.

    (a)

    $3 \div 2 =$

    (b)

    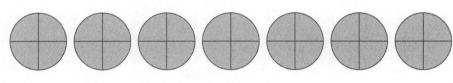

    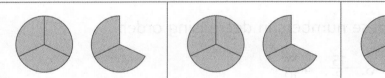

    $5 \div 3 =$

    (c)

    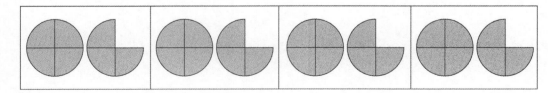

    $7 \div 4 =$

2. Change each improper fraction to a mixed number by division.

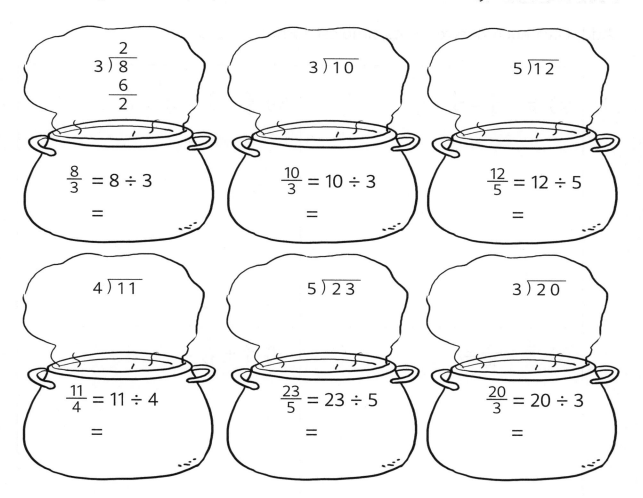

$3\overline{)8}$ with $\frac{2}{\ }$ and $\frac{6}{2}$

$\frac{8}{3} = 8 \div 3$

$=$

$3\overline{)10}$

$\frac{10}{3} = 10 \div 3$

$=$

$5\overline{)12}$

$\frac{12}{5} = 12 \div 5$

$=$

$4\overline{)11}$

$\frac{11}{4} = 11 \div 4$

$=$

$5\overline{)23}$

$\frac{23}{5} = 23 \div 5$

$=$

$3\overline{)20}$

$\frac{20}{3} = 20 \div 3$

$=$

3. Change each improper fraction to a whole number or a mixed number.

| (a) $\frac{8}{2} = 8 \div 2$        $2\overline{)8}$ | (b) $\frac{11}{5} = 11 \div 5$        $5\overline{)11}$ |
|---|---|
| (c) $\frac{17}{8} =$ | (d) $\frac{27}{3} =$ |

# EXERCISE 3

Add. Give each answer in its simplest form.

1.

(a) $\dfrac{7}{8} + \dfrac{3}{4} = \dfrac{7}{8} + \dfrac{\square}{8}$

$=$

(b) $\dfrac{2}{3} + \dfrac{4}{9} = \dfrac{\square}{9} + \dfrac{4}{9}$

$=$

(c) $\dfrac{4}{5} + \dfrac{3}{10} =$

(d) $\dfrac{3}{4} + \dfrac{7}{12} =$

(e) $\dfrac{5}{6} + \dfrac{2}{3} =$

(f) $\dfrac{1}{2} + \dfrac{9}{10} =$

2.

(a) $\dfrac{1}{6} + \dfrac{3}{4} = \dfrac{\boxed{\phantom{0}}}{12} + \dfrac{\boxed{\phantom{0}}}{12}$

$=$

(b) $\dfrac{5}{9} + \dfrac{1}{2} = \dfrac{\boxed{\phantom{0}}}{18} + \dfrac{\boxed{\phantom{0}}}{18}$

$=$

(c) $\dfrac{1}{2} + \dfrac{3}{5} =$

(d) $\dfrac{2}{5} + \dfrac{3}{4} =$

(e) $\dfrac{9}{10} + \dfrac{1}{6} =$

(f) $\dfrac{3}{10} + \dfrac{5}{6} =$

# EXERCISE 4

Subtract. Give each answer in its simplest form.

1.    (a) $\dfrac{7}{8} - \dfrac{3}{4} = \dfrac{7}{8} - \dfrac{\square}{8}$

           $=$

       (b) $\dfrac{5}{6} - \dfrac{1}{12} = \dfrac{\square}{12} - \dfrac{1}{12}$

              $=$

       (c) $\dfrac{9}{10} - \dfrac{1}{2} =$

       (d) $\dfrac{11}{12} - \dfrac{2}{3} =$

       (e) $1\dfrac{1}{2} - \dfrac{3}{4} =$

       (f) $1\dfrac{1}{10} - \dfrac{3}{5} =$

2.

(a) $\dfrac{1}{2} - \dfrac{1}{5} = \dfrac{\square}{10} - \dfrac{\square}{10}$

$=$

(b) $\dfrac{7}{12} - \dfrac{3}{8} = \dfrac{\square}{24} - \dfrac{\square}{24}$

$=$

(c) $\dfrac{3}{4} - \dfrac{3}{10} =$

(d) $\dfrac{9}{10} - \dfrac{3}{4} =$

(e) $1\dfrac{1}{5} - \dfrac{2}{3} =$

(f) $1\dfrac{1}{10} - \dfrac{1}{6} =$

# EXERCISE 5

Add. Give each answer in its simplest form.

1.

(a) $2\frac{3}{4} + 1\frac{1}{8} = 3\frac{3}{4} + \frac{1}{8}$

$= 3\frac{\square}{8} + \frac{1}{8}$

$=$

(b) $1\frac{5}{12} + 3\frac{1}{3} = 4\frac{5}{12} + \frac{1}{3}$

$= 4\frac{5}{12} + \frac{\square}{12}$

$=$

(c) $3\frac{7}{10} + 2\frac{2}{5} =$

(d) $2\frac{2}{3} + 2\frac{5}{12} =$

(e) $3\frac{7}{12} + 1\frac{3}{4} =$

(f) $1\frac{4}{5} + 2\frac{7}{10} =$

2.

(a) $2\frac{1}{5} + 1\frac{2}{3} = 3\frac{1}{5} + \frac{2}{3}$

$\quad\quad = 3\frac{\square}{15} + \frac{\square}{15}$

$\quad\quad =$

(b) $2\frac{3}{8} + 2\frac{1}{6} = 4\frac{3}{8} + \frac{1}{6}$

$\quad\quad = 4\frac{\square}{24} + \frac{\square}{24}$

$\quad\quad =$

(c) $1\frac{2}{5} + 5\frac{3}{4} =$

(d) $3\frac{1}{2} + 2\frac{7}{9} =$

(e) $2\frac{3}{10} + 2\frac{1}{6} =$

(f) $2\frac{5}{6} + 2\frac{9}{10} =$

# EXERCISE 6

Subtract. Give each answer in its simplest form.

1.

(a) $3\frac{7}{8} - 1\frac{1}{2} = 2\frac{7}{8} - \frac{1}{2}$

$= 2\frac{7}{8} - \frac{\square}{8}$

$=$

(b) $5\frac{4}{5} - 2\frac{1}{10} = 3\frac{4}{5} - \frac{1}{10}$

$= 3\frac{\square}{10} - \frac{\square}{10}$

$=$

(c) $4\frac{5}{6} - 2\frac{7}{12} =$

(d) $5\frac{11}{12} - 1\frac{3}{4} =$

(e) $4\frac{1}{9} - 2\frac{2}{3} =$

(f) $4\frac{1}{4} - 1\frac{5}{12} =$

2.

(a) $4\frac{1}{2} - 1\frac{2}{9} = 3\frac{1}{2} - \frac{2}{9}$

$\qquad = 3\frac{\square}{18} - \frac{\square}{18}$

$\qquad =$

(b) $3\frac{3}{4} - 1\frac{2}{3} = 2\frac{3}{4} - \frac{2}{3}$

$\qquad = 2\frac{\square}{12} - \frac{\square}{12}$

$\qquad =$

(c) $3\frac{5}{9} - 1\frac{1}{2} =$

(d) $4\frac{7}{8} - 2\frac{5}{12} =$

(e) $4\frac{1}{4} - 2\frac{5}{6} =$

(f) $4\frac{3}{10} - 3\frac{5}{6} =$

# EXERCISE 7

Multiply. Give each answer in its simplest form.

1.    (a)

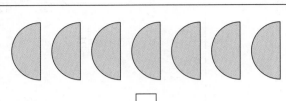

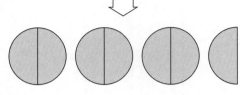

$\frac{1}{2} \times 7 =$

     (b)

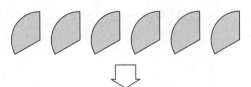

$\frac{1}{3} \times 6 =$

     (c)

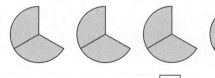

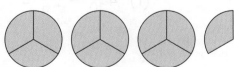

$\frac{2}{3} \times 5 =$

     (d)

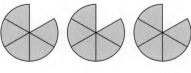

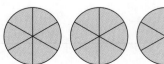

$\frac{5}{6} \times 3 =$

2.

| (a) $\frac{1}{3} \times 9 =$ | (b) $\frac{1}{2} \times 12 =$ |
|---|---|
| (c) $\frac{1}{4} \times 14 =$ | (d) $\frac{1}{6} \times 5 =$ |
| (e) $\frac{3}{5} \times 2 =$ | (f) $\frac{3}{4} \times 4 =$ |
| (g) $\frac{5}{8} \times 6 =$ | (h) $\frac{2}{3} \times 15 =$ |

# EXERCISE 8

1. (a) Multiply $\frac{1}{3}$ by 4.

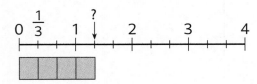

$$\frac{1}{3} \times 4 =$$

(b) Multiply $\frac{4}{5}$ by 3.

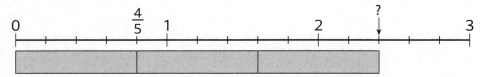

$$\frac{4}{5} \times 3 =$$

2. (a) Multiply 4 by $\frac{1}{3}$.

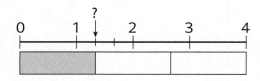

$$4 \times \frac{1}{3} =$$

(b) Multiply 5 by $\frac{3}{4}$.

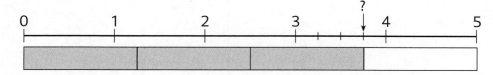

$$5 \times \frac{3}{4} =$$

3. Multiply. Give each answer in its simplest form.

| | | |
|---|---|---|
| (a) $8 \times \frac{1}{3} =$ | (b) $12 \times \frac{1}{2} =$ | (c) $14 \times \frac{1}{4} =$ |
| (d) $5 \times \frac{1}{6} =$ | (e) $2 \times \frac{3}{5} =$ | (f) $4 \times \frac{2}{5} =$ |
| (g) $\frac{1}{5} \times 6 =$ | (h) $\frac{4}{5} \times 10 =$ | (i) $\frac{2}{3} \times 4 =$ |

# EXERCISE 9

Find the value of each of the following.

1.  (a)

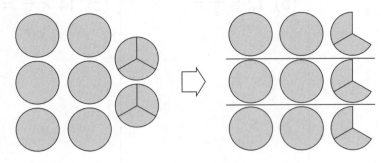

$\frac{1}{3}$ of 8 =

(b)

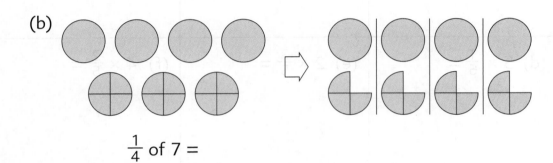

$\frac{1}{4}$ of 7 =

(c)

$\frac{5}{6}$ of 9 =

(d)

$\frac{3}{8}$ of 10 =

2.

| (a) $\frac{2}{3}$ of $7 = \frac{2}{3} \times 7$ <br><br> $=$ | (b) $\frac{3}{5}$ of $6 =$ |
|---|---|
| (c) $\frac{5}{6}$ of $5 =$ | (d) $\frac{5}{8}$ of $9 =$ |
| (e) $\frac{5}{9}$ of $3 =$ | (f) $\frac{3}{10}$ of $8 =$ |
| (g) $\frac{5}{6}$ of $10 =$ | (h) $\frac{7}{8}$ of $20 =$ |

Unit 3: Fractions

# EXERCISE 10

1. Find the equivalent measures.

| | |
|---|---|
| (a) $\frac{5}{8}$ day = ___ h<br><br>$\frac{5}{8}$ day = $\frac{5}{8}$ × 24 h<br><br>= | (b) $\frac{7}{10}$ m = ___ cm |
| (c) $\frac{9}{20}$ min = ___ s | (d) $\frac{3}{4}$ gal = ___ qt |
| (e) $\frac{3}{4}$ ft = ___ in. | (f) $\frac{9}{10}$ kg = ___ g |
| (g) $\frac{3}{5}$ km = ___ m | (h) $\frac{5}{6}$ h = ___ min |

2. Write each of the following in compound units.

(a) $2\frac{3}{5}$ m = 2 m _____ cm

$\frac{3}{5}$ m = $\frac{3}{5}$ × 100 cm

=

(b) $4\frac{7}{10}$ $\ell$ = 4 $\ell$ _____ ml

(c) $3\frac{1}{4}$ h = _____ h _____ min

(d) $2\frac{1}{2}$ days = _____ days _____ h

(e) $2\frac{2}{5}$ $\ell$ = _____ $\ell$ _____ ml

(f) $5\frac{1}{4}$ kg = _____ kg _____ g

(g) $4\frac{3}{4}$ lb = _____ lb _____ oz

(h) $3\frac{7}{8}$ km = _____ km _____ m

# EXERCISE 11

1. Find the equivalent measures.

| | |
|---|---|
| (a) $2\frac{1}{10}$ kg = _____ g<br><br>$\quad$ 2 kg =<br><br>$\quad \frac{1}{10}$ kg = $\frac{1}{10}$ × 1000 g<br><br>$\qquad$ =<br><br>$\quad 2\frac{1}{10}$ kg = | (b) $1\frac{1}{6}$ h = _____ min |
| (c) $2\frac{2}{3}$ years = _____ months | (d) $3\frac{1}{2}$ kg = _____ g |
| (e) $2\frac{1}{5}$ $\ell$ = _____ ml | (f) $2\frac{5}{6}$ min = _____ s |
| (g) $4\frac{3}{5}$ m = _____ cm | (h) $3\frac{4}{5}$ km = _____ m |

2. Brian jogs $3\frac{1}{8}$ km.

   Express $3\frac{1}{8}$ km in meters.

3. Peter practices the piano for $1\frac{3}{4}$ hours.
   Pablo practices for 125 minutes.
   Who practices for a longer time? How much longer?

4. Write >, < or = in each $\bigcirc$.

   (a) $1\frac{1}{2}$ ℓ $\bigcirc$ 1050 ml

   (b) $1\frac{2}{3}$ h $\bigcirc$ 100 min

   (c) $2\frac{1}{4}$ km $\bigcirc$ 2500 m

   (d) $1\frac{1}{20}$ m $\bigcirc$ 120 cm

   (e) $1\frac{3}{4}$ ft $\bigcirc$ 20 in.

   (f) $1\frac{1}{4}$ ℓ $\bigcirc$ 1500 ml

   (g) $1\frac{1}{3}$ days $\bigcirc$ 30 h

   (h) $1\frac{2}{3}$ years $\bigcirc$ 20 months

   (i) $1\frac{4}{5}$ kg $\bigcirc$ 1400 g

   (j) $2\frac{1}{4}$ qt $\bigcirc$ 10 c

## EXERCISE 12

1.  Express 8 months as a fraction of 1 year.   1 year = 12 months

    $$\frac{8}{12} =$$

---

2.  Express 95 cm as a fraction of 1 m.

---

3.  Express 45 minutes as a fraction of 1 hour.

---

4.  Express 15 cents as a fraction of $1.

---

5.  Express 650 g as a fraction of 1 kg.

6. Express 40 minutes as a fraction of 2 hours.

$$\frac{40}{120} =$$

2 h = 2 × 60 min

7. Express 8 in. as a fraction of 3 ft.

8. What fraction of $3 is 90 cents?

9. Mrs. King bought 2 kg of flour. She used 750 g to bake some bread.
   (a) What fraction of the flour did she use?
   (b) What fraction of the flour was left?

# EXERCISE 13

1. There are 50 oranges in a box. $\frac{3}{10}$ of them are rotten. How many oranges are **not** rotten?

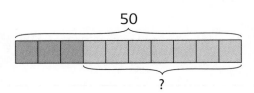

2. Petrina spent $\frac{2}{5}$ of her money and had $60 left. How much money did she have at first?

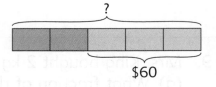

3. After spending \$30 on a dress, Mary had $\frac{3}{8}$ of her money left. How much money did she have at first?

---

4. $\frac{4}{7}$ of a group of children are boys. If there are 18 more boys than girls, how many children are there altogether?

1. A tank is $\frac{4}{5}$ full of water. If 40 gal more water are needed to fill the tank completely, find the **capacity** of the tank.

---

2. There are 1400 students in a school. $\frac{1}{4}$ of the students wear eyeglasses. $\frac{2}{7}$ of those who wear eyeglasses are boys. How many boys in the school wear eyeglasses?

3. Larry spent $\frac{1}{2}$ of his money on a camera and another $\frac{1}{8}$ on a radio. The camera cost $120 more than the radio. How much money did he have at first?

4. Mrs. Ricci had $480. She used $\frac{2}{3}$ of it to buy an electric fan. She also bought a tea set for $60. How much money did she have left?

# REVIEW 3

1. What is the missing number in each of the following regular number patterns?

    (a) 10,780,  12,780,  14,780, ⬚ , 18,780

    (b) 20,945,  20,445, ⬚ ,  19,445,  18,945

    (c) $1\frac{1}{4}$,  $1\frac{1}{2}$,  $1\frac{3}{4}$,  2, ⬚

    (d) $4\frac{2}{3}$,  $4\frac{1}{3}$,  4, ⬚ ,  $3\frac{1}{3}$

2. What is the missing number in each ⬚ ?

    (a) 67 × ⬚ = 67,000

    (b) ⬚ × 3040 = 30,400

    (c) 50,800 ÷ ⬚ = 508

    (d) 76,000 ÷ ⬚ = 7600

    (e) 42 × 23 = (40 × 23) + (2 × ⬚ )

3. (a) Which one of the following numbers is a common multiple of 4, 5 and 10?

    4,  5,  50,  100                                    ⬚

    (b) Which one of the following numbers is a common factor of 28 and 84?

    3,  8,  28,  84                                     ⬚

4. (a) Round 3,090,456 to the nearest 100,000.        ⬚

    (b) Round 49,958 to the nearest 100.              ⬚

5. Find the value of each of the following.
   (a)  240 + 60 × 5

   (b)  320 − 80 + 120 ÷ 6

   (c)  (40 + 24) ÷ 4 × 3

   (d)  $11^3$

6. (a) Write 8 ÷ 18 as a fraction in its simplest form.

   (b) Write $\frac{46}{12}$ as a mixed number in its simplest form.

7. (a) How many minutes are there in 3 hours?

   (b) How many milliliters are there in $2\frac{1}{2}$ liters?

   (c) How many months are there in $2\frac{1}{3}$ years?

8. (a) The difference between 5 and $2\frac{1}{4}$ is [          ].

   (b) The product of $\frac{5}{12}$ and 4 is [          ].

9. (a) Express 9 months as a fraction of 2 years.

   (b) Express 50 minutes as a fraction of 3 hours.

10. Rewrite the prime factorization using exponents.
    2 × 3 × 11 × 3 × 19 × 19

11. Find the prime factorization of 82.

12. (a) What fraction of 3 lb is 8 oz?

    (b) What fraction of 2 gal is 3 qt?

    (c) What fraction of 2 qt is 4 c?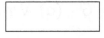

13. Find the missing number in each ▢.

    (a) $\frac{1}{8} \times 3 + \frac{1}{8} + \frac{1}{8} + \frac{1}{8} = \frac{1}{8} \times$ ▢

    (b) ▢ $\times \frac{3}{4} = 3$

14. If 5 pears cost $3, find the cost of 20 pears.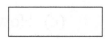

15. If 100 g of prawns cost $2, find the cost of $\frac{1}{2}$ kg of prawns.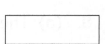

16. A ribbon is $\frac{3}{4}$ ft long. Express $\frac{3}{4}$ ft in inches.

17. Mrs. Garcia had 6 lb of flour. She used $\frac{1}{5}$ of it to make bread. How many pounds of flour did she have left?

18. Write >, < or = in each ◯.

    (a) $\frac{4}{5}$ m ◯ 80 cm        (b) $3\frac{1}{2}$ years ◯ 3 years 5 months

    (c) $2\frac{1}{10}$ kg ◯ 2001 g        (d) 350 ml ◯ 3 ℓ 50 ml

19. (a) 4 km is [＿＿＿＿] m more than 3 km 650 m.

    (b) 290 ml × 4 is equal to [＿＿＿] ℓ [＿＿＿] ml.

20. Lynn ordered a table which cost $150 and 4 chairs which cost $24 each. She paid a deposit of $50. How much did she have to pay when the table and chairs were delivered?

# EXERCISE 1

1. Find the value of each of the following.

| | |
|---|---|
| **(a)** 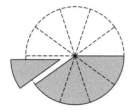 $\frac{1}{5}$ of $\frac{1}{2}$ = | $\frac{1}{5} \times \frac{1}{2} = \frac{1 \times 1}{5 \times 2}$ <br><br> = |
| **(b)** 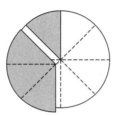 $\frac{3}{4}$ of $\frac{1}{2}$ = | $\frac{3}{4} \times \frac{1}{2} =$ |
| **(c)** 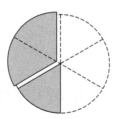 $\frac{2}{3}$ of $\frac{1}{2}$ = | $\frac{2}{3} \times \frac{1}{2} =$ |
| **(d)** 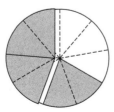 $\frac{2}{3}$ of $\frac{2}{3}$ = | $\frac{2}{3} \times \frac{2}{3} =$ |

2. Mrs. Smith bought $\frac{5}{6}$ lb of meat. She cooked $\frac{2}{3}$ of it. How much meat did she cook?

$$\frac{2}{3} \times \frac{5}{6} =$$

3. A rectangle measures $\frac{3}{4}$ yd by $\frac{2}{5}$ yd. Find its area.

4. Susan spent $\frac{3}{5}$ of her money on a calculator and $\frac{2}{3}$ of the remainder on a pen. What fraction of her money did she have left?

# EXERCISE 2

1. Multiply.

| | |
|---|---|
| (a) $\dfrac{4}{9} \times \dfrac{1}{2} =$ | (b) $\dfrac{1}{4} \times \dfrac{3}{8} =$ |
| (c) $\dfrac{1}{5} \times \dfrac{3}{4} =$ | (d) $\dfrac{5}{6} \times \dfrac{2}{3} =$ |
| (e) $\dfrac{4}{5} \times \dfrac{5}{8} =$ | (f) $\dfrac{4}{9} \times \dfrac{3}{10} =$ |
| (g) $\dfrac{9}{10} \times \dfrac{5}{6} =$ | (h) $\dfrac{8}{3} \times \dfrac{6}{7} =$ |

2. Find the answers by following the arrows.

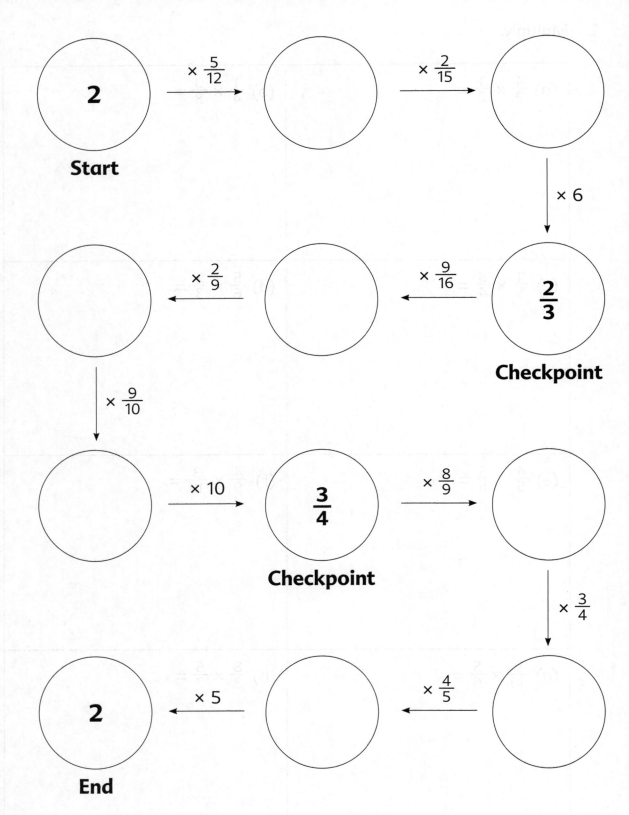

Unit 4: Multiply and Divide Fractions

# EXERCISE 3

1.  Tracy bought 120 eggs. She fried $\frac{2}{3}$ of them and boiled $\frac{1}{4}$ of the remainder. How many eggs did she have left?

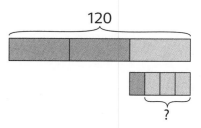

2.  Mr. Ramirez had $600. He gave $\frac{3}{5}$ of it to his wife and spent $\frac{3}{8}$ of the remainder. How much did he spend?

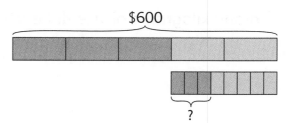

3. Lindsey made 400 tarts. She sold $\frac{3}{5}$ of them in the morning and $\frac{1}{4}$ of the remainder in the afternoon. How many tarts did she sell in the afternoon?

4. Sam packed 42 kg of rice into one big bag and 6 small ones which were of the same size. The big bag contained $\frac{3}{7}$ of the rice. How many kilograms of rice did each small bag contain?

# EXERCISE 4

1. Christian made some pancakes. She sold $\frac{3}{5}$ of them in the morning and $\frac{1}{4}$ of the remainder in the afternoon. If she had 300 pancakes left, how many pancakes did she make?

2. Mrs. Klein made some fruit buns. She sold $\frac{3}{5}$ of them in the morning and $\frac{1}{4}$ of the remainder in the afternoon. If she sold 200 more fruit buns in the morning than in the afternoon, how many fruit buns did she make?

3. Alex spent $\frac{1}{3}$ of his pocket money on a toy airplane and $\frac{2}{3}$ of the remainder on a toy robot. He had $20 left. How much did he spend altogether?

4. John spent $\frac{2}{3}$ of his money on a pen and a calculator. The calculator cost 3 times as much as the pen. If the calculator cost $24, how much money did he have left?

# EXERCISE 5

1. Find the value of each of the following.

(a) $\frac{1}{4} \div 2 = \frac{1}{4} \times \frac{1}{2}$

$=$

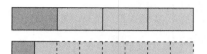

$\frac{1}{2}$ of $\frac{1}{4} =$

(b) $\frac{2}{3} \div 4 = \frac{2}{3} \times \frac{1}{4}$

$=$

$\frac{1}{4}$ of $\frac{2}{3} =$

(c) $\frac{2}{3} \div 3 = \frac{2}{3} \times \frac{1}{3}$

$=$

$\frac{1}{3}$ of $\frac{2}{3} =$

(d) $\frac{4}{5} \div 8 = \frac{4}{5} \times \frac{1}{8}$

$=$

$\frac{1}{8}$ of $\frac{4}{5} =$

2. Divide.

| | |
|---|---|
| (a) $\frac{3}{4} \div 2 =$ | (b) $\frac{8}{9} \div 4 =$ |
| (c) $\frac{5}{6} \div 5 =$ | (d) $\frac{3}{5} \div 9 =$ |
| (e) $\frac{4}{5} \div 2 =$ | (f) $\frac{5}{7} \div 6 =$ |
| (g) $\frac{5}{8} \div 3 =$ | (h) $\frac{4}{9} \div 10 =$ |

# EXERCISE 6

1.  Find the answers by following the arrows.

    (a)

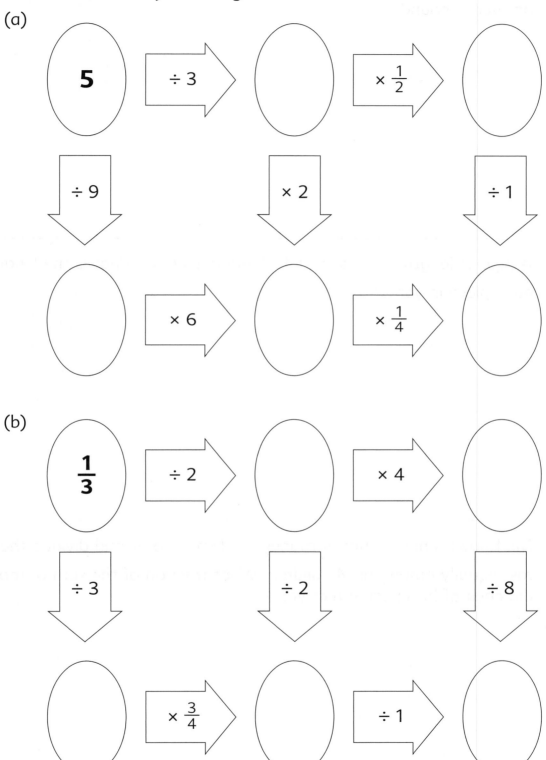

    (b)

2. Mrs. Campbell used $\frac{3}{5}$ lb of sugar in 6 days. If she used the same amount each day, how much sugar did she use each day? Give your answer in pounds.

---

3. A pipe of length $\frac{1}{2}$ yd is cut into 5 equal pieces. What is the length of each piece in yards?

---

4. Mr. Knowles had a sum of money. He kept $\frac{1}{3}$ of it and divided the rest equally among his 4 children. What fraction of the sum of money did each of his children receive?

# EXERCISE 7

1.  Divide. Then use the pictures to check your answers.

(a)

$3 \div \frac{1}{4} = 3 \times 4$

$=$

3 wholes can be divided into _____ quarters.

(b)

$2 \div \frac{1}{5} = 2 \times$

$=$

2 wholes can be divided into _____ fifths.

(c)

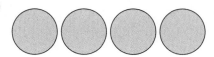  

$4 \div \frac{1}{2} = 4 \times$

$=$

4 wholes can be divided into _____ halves.

(d)

$3 \div \frac{1}{6} = 3 \times$

$=$

3 wholes can be divided into _____ sixths.

2. Divide.

| | |
|---|---|
| (a) $3 \div \frac{1}{2} = 3 \times 2$<br><br>$= $ | (b) $3 \div \frac{1}{5} = 3 \times$<br><br>$= $ |
| (c) $4 \div \frac{1}{3} = $ | (d) $4 \div \frac{1}{4} = $ |
| (e) $5 \div \frac{1}{5} = $ | (f) $6 \div \frac{1}{3} = $ |
| (g) $1 \div \frac{1}{8} = $ | (h) $7 \div \frac{1}{6} = $ |

# EXERCISE 8

1.  Divide.

| | |
|---|---|
| (a) $\frac{1}{3} \div \frac{1}{3} =$ | (b) $\frac{1}{2} \div \frac{1}{6} =$ |
| (c) $\frac{1}{6} \div \frac{1}{4} =$ | (d) $\frac{4}{5} \div \frac{1}{2} =$ |
| (e) $\frac{2}{4} \div \frac{1}{4} =$ | (f) $\frac{8}{9} \div \frac{1}{4} =$ |
| (g) $\frac{3}{4} \div \frac{1}{2} =$ | (h) $\frac{2}{3} \div \frac{1}{6} =$ |

# EXERCISE 9

1. Divide.

| | |
|---|---|
| (a) $1 \div \frac{3}{4} =$ | (b) $2 \div \frac{3}{4} =$ |
| (c) $10 \div \frac{5}{8} =$ | (d) $10 \div \frac{3}{5} =$ |
| (e) $4 \div \frac{4}{5} =$ | (f) $6 \div \frac{3}{4} =$ |
| (g) $8 \div \frac{4}{5} =$ | (h) $5 \div \frac{3}{8} =$ |

# EXERCISE 10

1. Divide.

| | |
|---|---|
| (a) $\frac{1}{2} \div \frac{2}{3} =$ | (b) $\frac{2}{3} \div \frac{5}{6} =$ |
| (c) $\frac{1}{8} \div \frac{3}{4} =$ | (d) $\frac{4}{9} \div \frac{2}{3} =$ |
| (e) $\frac{2}{5} \div \frac{3}{10} =$ | (f) $\frac{2}{7} \div \frac{3}{5} =$ |
| (g) $\frac{3}{8} \div \frac{3}{4} =$ | (h) $\frac{5}{9} \div \frac{2}{3} =$ |

# EXERCISE 11

1. A shopkeeper had 150 lb of rice. He sold $\frac{2}{5}$ of it and packed the remainder equally into 5 bags. Find the weight of the rice in each bag.

2. Peter had 400 stamps. $\frac{5}{8}$ of them are U.S. stamps and the rest are Canadian stamps. He gave $\frac{1}{5}$ of the U.S. stamps to his friend. How many stamps did he have left?

3. Kyle gave $\frac{2}{7}$ of his money to his wife and spent $\frac{3}{5}$ of the remainder. If he had $300 left, how much money did he have at first?

4. $\frac{2}{3}$ of the beads in a box are red, $\frac{1}{4}$ are yellow and the rest are blue. There are 42 more red beads than blue beads. How many beads are there altogether?

# EXERCISE 12

1.  Lucy spent $\frac{3}{5}$ of her money on a handbag. She spent the rest of the money on a dress and a belt. The handbag cost twice as much as the dress. The dress cost $20 more than the belt. How much money did she have at first?

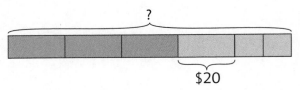

2. Gary spent $48 on a watch. He spent $\frac{1}{3}$ of the remainder on a pen. If he still had $\frac{1}{2}$ of his money left, how much money did he have at first?

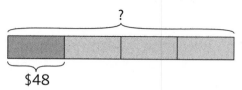

3. After giving $\frac{1}{3}$ of his money to his wife and $\frac{1}{4}$ of it to his mother, Mr. Li still had $600 left. How much money did he give to his mother?

4. Lucy spent $\frac{3}{5}$ of her money on a purse. She spent the remainder on 3 T-shirts which cost $4 each.  How much did the purse cost?

# REVIEW 4

1.  Write >, < or = in each $\bigcirc$.

    (a) $4\frac{1}{2}$ $\bigcirc$ $\frac{42}{4}$

    (b) $3\frac{1}{7}$ $\bigcirc$ $\frac{31}{7}$

    (c) $\frac{34}{8}$ $\bigcirc$ $4\frac{1}{4}$

    (d) $10\frac{1}{3}$ $\bigcirc$ $\frac{10}{3}$

2.  Find the value of each of the following.

    (a) $2\frac{3}{8} + \frac{7}{12}$

    (b) $4\frac{1}{3} - 1\frac{8}{9}$

    (c) $\frac{7}{9} \times \frac{3}{4}$

    (d) $36 \times \frac{5}{9}$

    (e) $\frac{2}{3} \div \frac{5}{6}$

    (f) $3 \div \frac{1}{8}$

3.  Fill in the blanks.

    (a) $4\frac{1}{2}$ h = [            ] h [            ] min

    (b) $2\frac{1}{4}$ years = [            ] years [            ] months

    (c) $3\frac{9}{10}$ m = [            ] m [            ] cm

    (d) $5\frac{3}{10}$ kg = [            ] kg [            ] g

4. (a) Which is longer, $\frac{4}{5}$ m or 85 cm?

   (b) Which is longer, $1\frac{2}{3}$ years or 17 months?

   (c) Which is heavier, $2\frac{1}{10}$ kg or 2001 g?

   (d) Which is more, 350 ml or 3 $\ell$ 50 ml?

5. The following figure is made up of congruent rectangles. What fraction of the figure is shaded?

6. Write >, < or = in each ◯.

   (a) 45,800 × 3 ◯ (45,000 × 3) + (800 × 3)

   (b) 65,000,000 ÷ 1000 ◯ 650,000

   (c) 8000 + 50 ◯ 8000 − 100

   (d) 450 ÷ 2 ◯ 45 × 2

   (e) 64 ◯ $2^8$

7. If 2 liters of a liquid weigh 600 g, then 3 liters of the liquid weigh [     ] g.

8. Lihua bought 5 packets of white envelopes and 3 packets of brown envelopes. There were 112 envelopes in each packet. How many envelopes did she buy altogether?

9. Robert packed 1320 stickers into packets of 22 each. He sold all the stickers at $2 per packet. How much money did he make?

10. Lily has been working for $6\frac{1}{4}$ years and Susan has been working for $2\frac{1}{2}$ years. Lily has been working ⬚ years ⬚ months longer than Susan.

11. 64 children attended a computer course. $\frac{5}{8}$ of them were girls. How many more girls than boys were there? ⬚

12. Arrange the following numbers in decreasing order.
    $\frac{9}{4}$, $2\frac{1}{12}$, $2\frac{1}{2}$, $\frac{12}{11}$

    ⬚

13. Which one is the following is nearest to 4?
    $3\frac{1}{8}$, $3\frac{11}{12}$, $4\frac{9}{10}$, $4\frac{4}{5}$    ⬚

14. Mrs. Harris bought 4 pounds of meat with $\frac{2}{5}$ of her money. She still had $24 left. How much did 1 pound of meat cost?

15. Brian bought 54 tangerines. He gave away $\frac{2}{3}$ of them and ate $\frac{1}{6}$ of the remainder. How many tangerines did he have left?

16. Ali sold 5 oven toasters and 3 rice cookers for $500. If a rice cooker cost $20 less than an oven toaster, find the cost of a rice cooker.

# EXERCISE 1

1. Find the area of each figure. Then complete the table below.

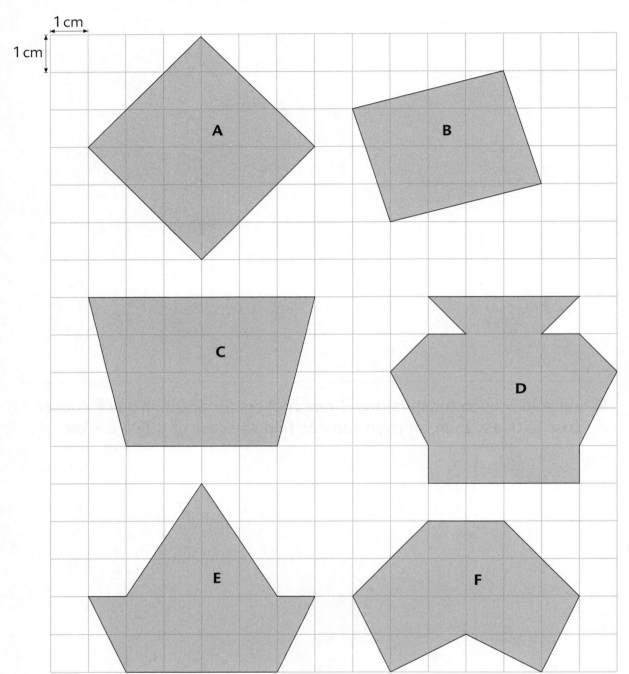

| Figure | A | B | C | D | E | F |
|--------|---|---|---|---|---|---|
| Area   |   |   |   |   |   |   |

2. Find the area of each triangle. Then complete the table below.

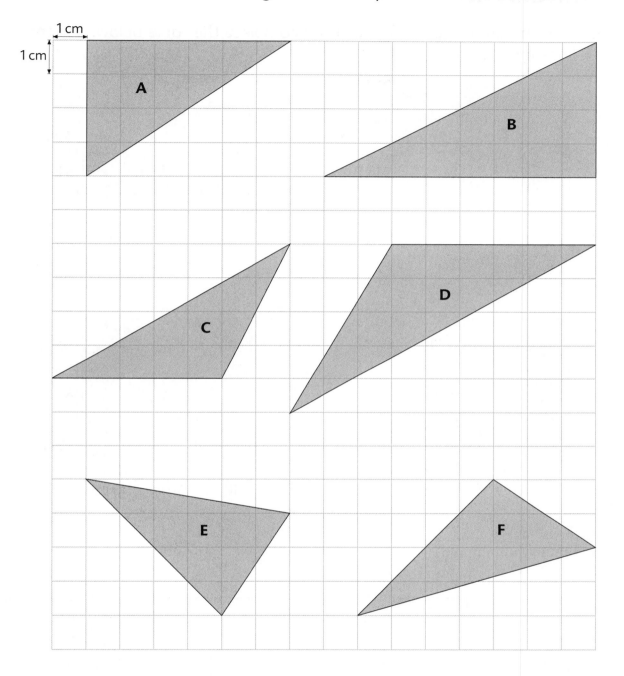

| Figure | A | B | C | D | E | F |
|--------|---|---|---|---|---|---|
| Area |   |   |   |   |   |   |

# EXERCISE 2

1. Find the area of each figure. Then complete the table below. (All the lines meet at right angles.)

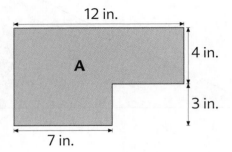

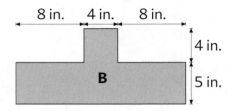

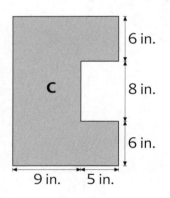

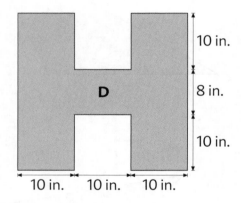

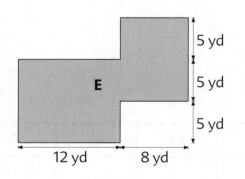

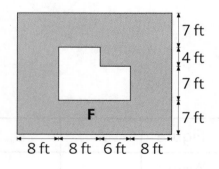

| Figure | A | B | C | D | E | F |
|--------|---|---|---|---|---|---|
| Area   |   |   |   |   |   |   |

# EXERCISE 3

1.  Draw the height to the given base of each triangle.

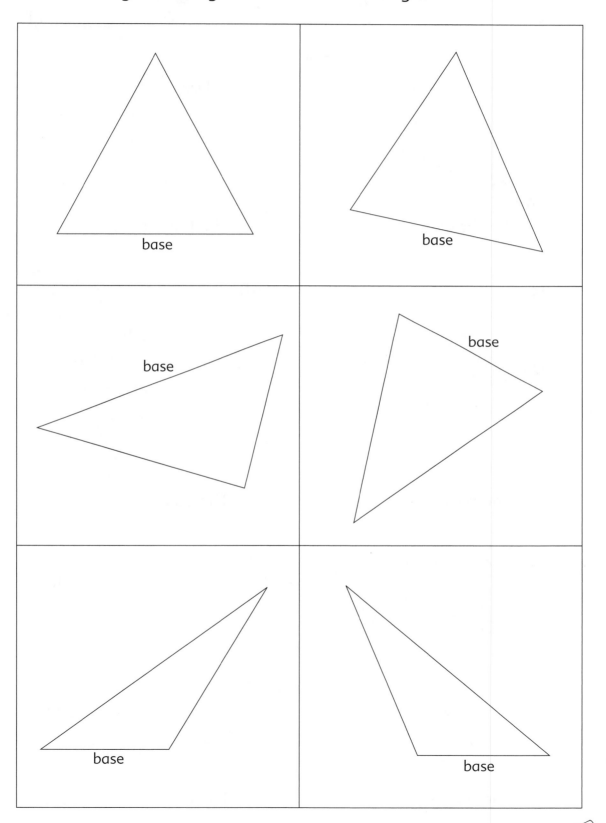

2. For each of the following triangles, name the **base** which is related to the given height.

(a)

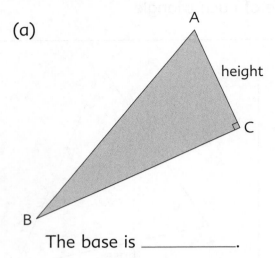

The base is _____.

(b)

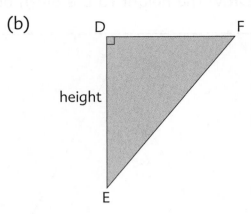

The base is _____.

(c)

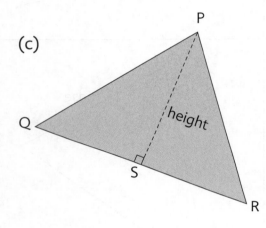

The base is _____.

(d)

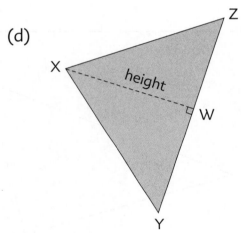

The base is _____.

(e)

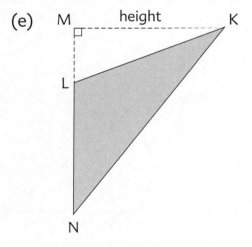

The base is _____.

(f)

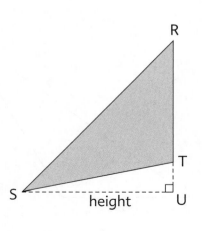

The base is _____.

Find the area of each triangle.

3. (a)

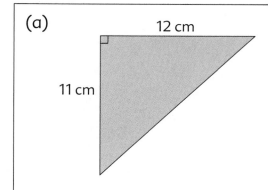
12 cm

11 cm

Area of the triangle
= $\frac{1}{2}$ × 12 × 11

=

(b)

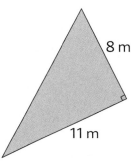
8 m

11 m

(c)

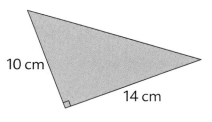
10 cm

14 cm

(d)

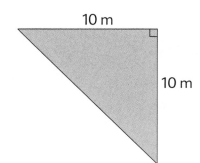
10 m

10 m

4.

(a)

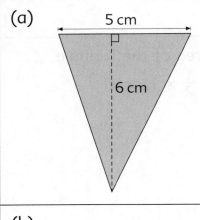

5 cm

6 cm

Area of the triangle

=

(b)

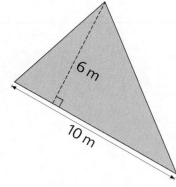

6 m

10 m

(c)

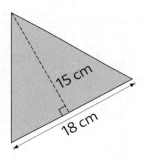

15 cm

18 cm

(d)

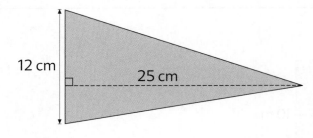

12 cm

25 cm

# EXERCISE 4

Find the area of each shaded triangle.

1.

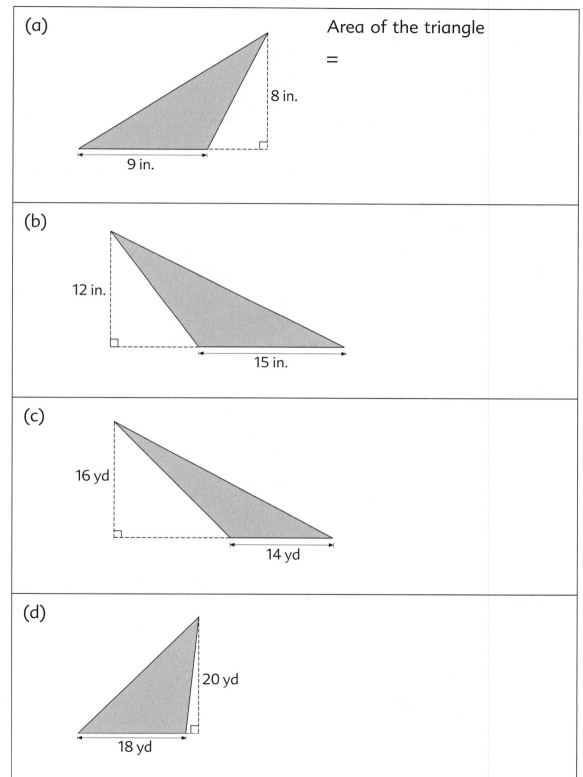

(a)

Area of the triangle

=

8 in.

9 in.

(b)

12 in.

15 in.

(c)

16 yd

14 yd

(d)

20 yd

18 yd

2. Find the area of each shaded triangle.

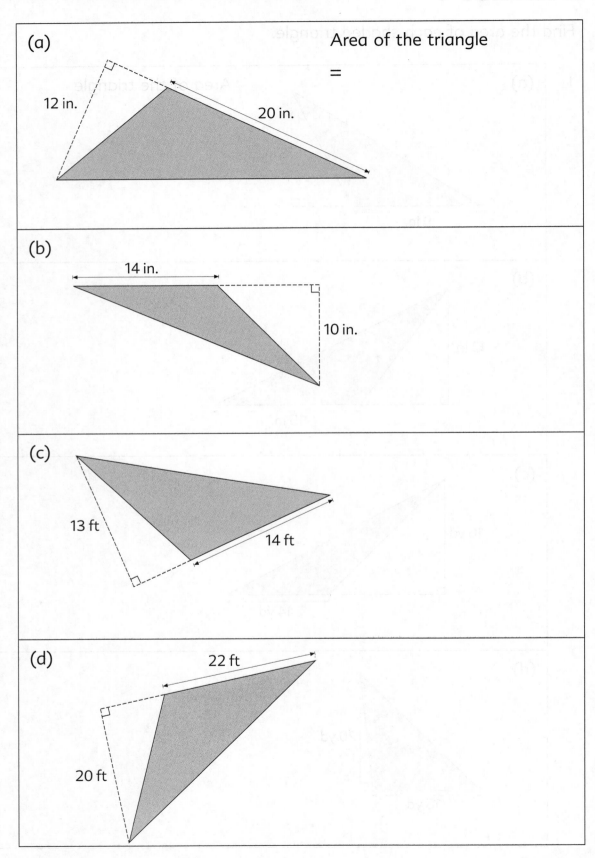

(a)

12 in.

20 in.

Area of the triangle

=

(b)

14 in.

10 in.

(c)

13 ft

14 ft

(d)

22 ft

20 ft

3.  Find the area of each shaded triangle. Then complete the table and answer the questions below.

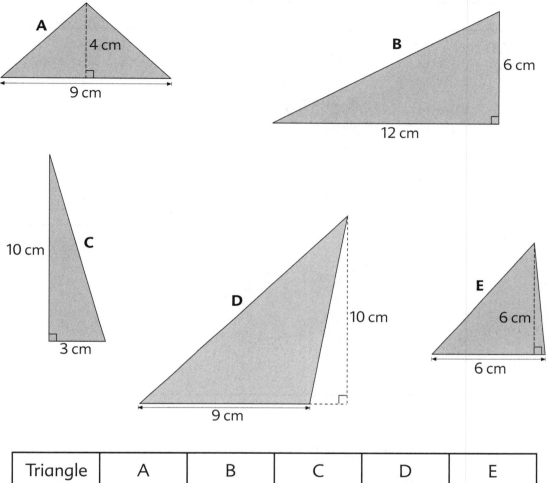

| Triangle | A | B | C | D | E |
|----------|---|---|---|---|---|
| Area     |   |   |   |   |   |

(a) Which triangle has the largest area?

(b) Which triangle has the smallest area?

(c) What is the difference in area between the largest triangle and the smallest triangle?

(d) Which triangle is twice as large as Triangle A?

(e) Which triangles have the same area?

# EXERCISE 5

1. Find the area of each shaded triangle.

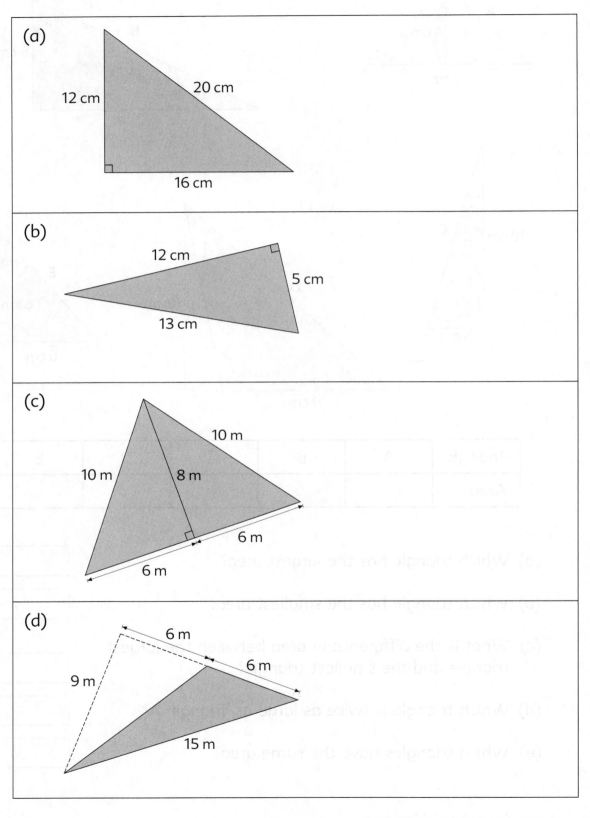

(a)

12 cm

20 cm

16 cm

(b)

12 cm

5 cm

13 cm

(c)

10 m

10 m

8 m

6 m

6 m

(d)

6 m

6 m

9 m

15 m

Unit 5: Perimeter, Area and Surface Area

2. Find the shaded area of each rectangle.

(a)

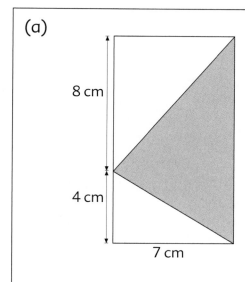

8 cm

4 cm

7 cm

(b)

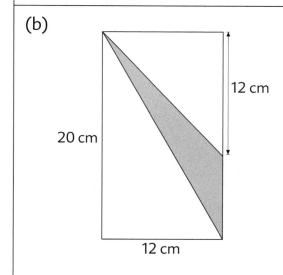

12 cm

20 cm

12 cm

(c)

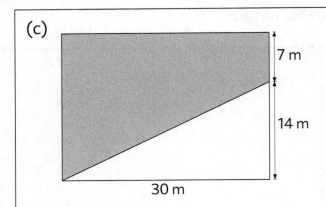

7 m

14 m

30 m

(d)

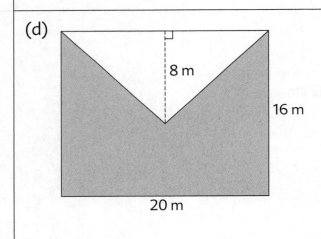

8 m

16 m

20 m

# EXERCISE 6

1.  Draw a different polygon with the same area.

    (a)

    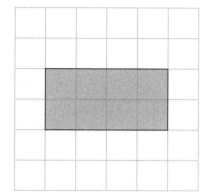 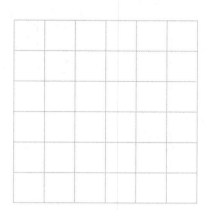

    (b)

    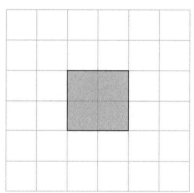 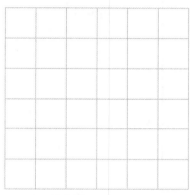

    (c)

    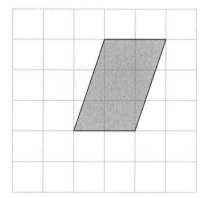 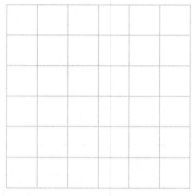

    (d)

    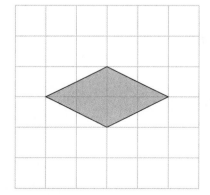 

2. Find the area of the figures.

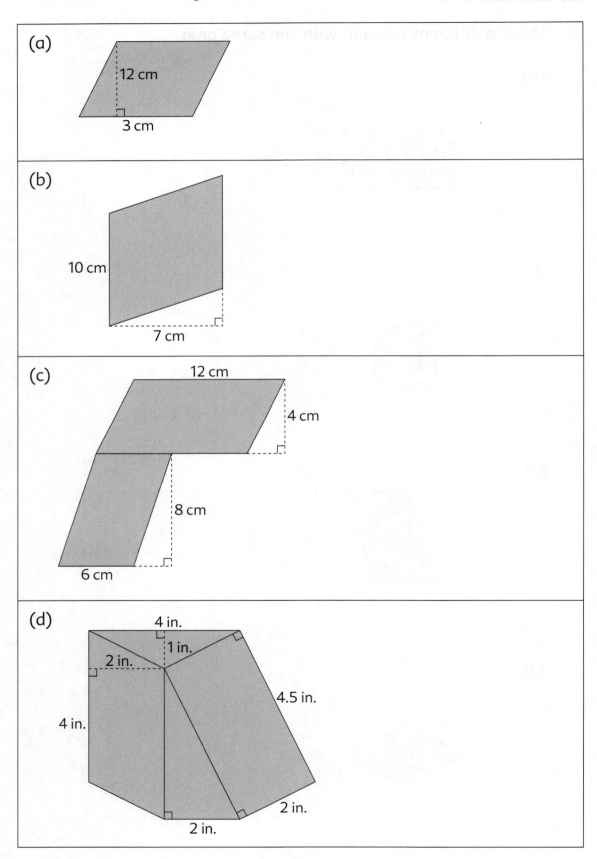

(a)

12 cm

3 cm

(b)

10 cm

7 cm

(c)

12 cm

4 cm

8 cm

6 cm

(d)

4 in.

1 in.

2 in.

4.5 in.

4 in.

2 in.

2 in.

# EXERCISE 7

1. Find the surface area of the following prisms.

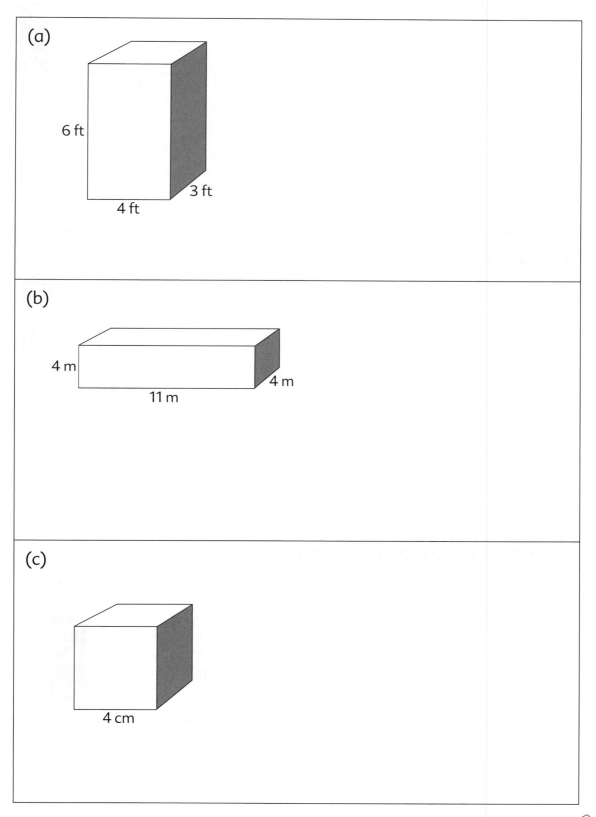

(a)

6 ft

3 ft

4 ft

(b)

4 m

11 m

4 m

(c)

4 cm

2. Find the surface area of a box with length 12 in., and width and height both of 4 in. each.

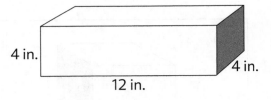

4 in.

12 in.

4 in.

3. Find the area of a cube with edge 5 cm.

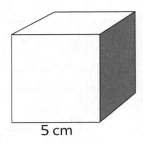

5 cm

4. Find the surface area of the box.

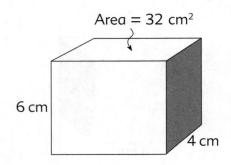

Area = 32 cm²

6 cm

4 cm

# REVIEW 5

1. Find the value of
   (a) $27 + 96 \div 12 \div 4$

   (b) $(45 + 27) \div (17 - 8)$

   (c) $48 + 12 + 37$

   (d) $36 + 18 - 19$

   (e) $51 - 35 + 18$

2. Find the prime factorization of 54.

3. Write in feet and inches.
   (a) 18 in.

   (b) 28 in.

   (c) 57 in.

4. (a) 4 h 54 min = ⬚ min

   (b) 3 m 5 cm = ⬚ cm

   (c) 5 kg 500 g = ⬚ g

   (d) 2050 g = ⬚ kg ⬚ g

   (e) 30 months = ⬚ years ⬚ months

5. Water is poured equally into 4 containers. Each container has 5 c of water. How many quarts of water are there in the four containers?

6. Mrs. Anderson bought 5 yd of cloth. She used the cloth to make 12 napkins of the same size. How much cloth did she use for each napkin? (Give the answer in feet.)

7. Adam poured 4 qt of milk equally into 5 jugs. How much milk was there in each jug? (Give the answer in quarts.)

8. A crate of strawberries weighing 8 lb was divided into 12 equal shares. What was the weight of each share? (Give the answer in ounces as a mixed number.)

9. A cook used $2\frac{1}{4}$ gal of oil last week. Express $2\frac{1}{4}$ gal in gallons and cups.

10. Mrs. Goldberg used 8.7 ft of lace for 5 pillow cases. If she used an equal length of lace for each pillow case, how much lace did she use for each pillow case? (Give the answer in feet.)

11. The area of a square is 81 in.$^2$. Find its perimeter.

12. Emily bought a bag of candies which weighed 1 lb 11 oz. She gave away 15 oz of candy. How many ounces of candy was left?

13. Find the surface area of a cube of length 6 in.

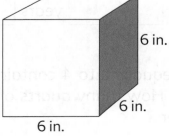

6 in.

6 in.

6 in.

14. Ryan drinks 2 c of milk a day. How much milk does he drink in three weeks? (Give the answer in quarts and cups.)

15. Multiply in compound units. Give the answer in compound units.

(a) 3 yd 2 ft × 7 = [          ] yd [          ] ft

(b) 5 lb 14 oz × 3 = [          ] lb [          ] oz

(c) 4 gal 3 qt × 5 = [          ] gal [          ] qt

(d) 2 ft 11 in. × 2 = [          ] ft [          ] in.

16. A rope was cut into three equal pieces. Each piece was 1 ft 6 in. long. What was the length of the rope? (Give the answer in feet and inches.)

17. Find the value of the following.

(a) $\frac{1}{3}$ of 24 yd

(b) $\frac{4}{5}$ of 35 in.

(c) $1\frac{1}{2}$ of 14 oz

(d) $\frac{5}{6}$ of 12 gal

18. Find the area of the figure.

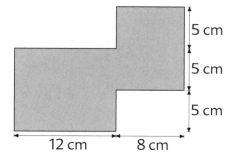

5 cm

5 cm

5 cm

12 cm        8 cm

19. The figure is made up of 2-cm squares.

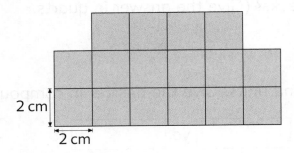

(a) Find the area of the figure.

(b) Find the perimeter of the figure.

20. Draw a straight line to divide the figure into two parts of equal area.

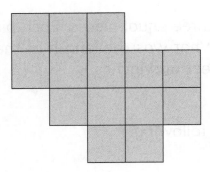

21. The figure is made up of two parallelograms. Find its area.

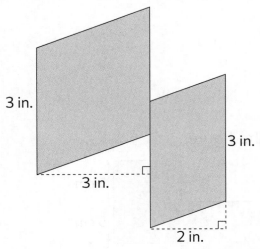

22. If the square has the same perimeter as the rectangle, find the area of the square.

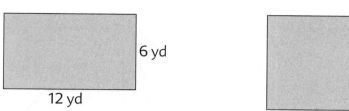

6 yd

12 yd

23. What fraction of the rectangle is shaded?

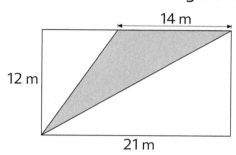

14 m

12 m

21 m

24. Find the shaded area of each of the rectangles.

(a)

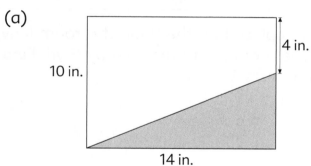

4 in.

10 in.

14 in.

(b)

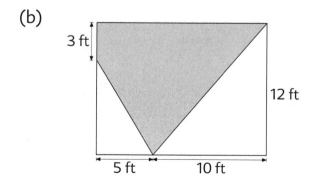

3 ft

12 ft

5 ft    10 ft

25. The area of the square is the same as the area of the triangle. Find the perimeter of the square.

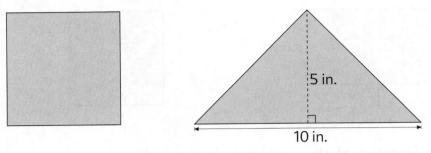

5 in.

10 in.

26. A rectangular piece of carpet is placed on the floor of a room leaving a margin of 1 yd around it. The room measures 7 yd by 6 yd. Find the cost of the carpet if 1 yd$^2$ of it costs $75.

# EXERCISE 1

1.

    (a) The ratio of the number of tables to the number of chairs is

    _____ : _____.

    (b) The ratio of the number of chairs to the number of tables is

    _____ : _____.

---

2. (a) The ratio of the number of triangles to the number of squares is

    _____ : _____.

  (b) The ratio of the number of squares to the number of triangles is

    _____ : _____.

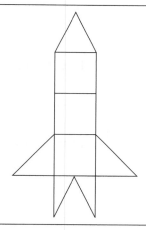

---

3.

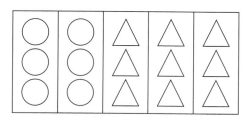

    (a) The ratio of the number of circles to the number of triangles is

    _____ : _____.

    (b) The ratio of the number of triangles to the number of circles is

    _____ : _____.

4.

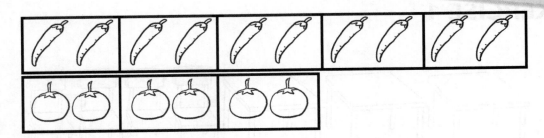

(a) The ratio of the number of peppers to the number of tomatoes is

_____ : _____.

(b) The ratio of the number of tomatoes to the number of peppers is

_____ : _____.

5.  A

B

(a) The ratio of the length of Ribbon A to the length of Ribbon B is

_____ : _____.

(b) The ratio of the length of Ribbon B to the length of Ribbon A is

_____ : _____.

6.

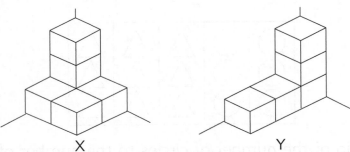

X                          Y

(a) The ratio of the volume of Solid X to the volume of Solid Y is

_____ : _____.

(b) The ratio of the volume of Solid Y to the volume of Solid X is

_____ : _____.

# EXERCISE 2

1. Write each ratio in its simplest form.

   (a) John saves $12 and David saves $30.
       The ratio of John's savings to David's savings is

       _____ : _____ .

   (b) Mark bought 15 lb of rice and 9 lb of sugar.
       The ratio of the weight of sugar to the weight of rice is

       _____ : _____ .

2. Write each ratio in the simplest form.

| | | | |
|---|---|---|---|
| 6 : 9 = | : | 12 : 4 = | : |
| 6 : 24 = | : | 6 : 10 = | : |
| 25 : 15 = | : | 8 : 4 = | : |
| 15 : 18 = | : | 16 : 20 = | : |
| 20 : 40 = | : | 30 : 24 = | : |

3. Write the missing numbers.

   (a) 2 : 1 = 10 : _____      (b) 3 : 12 = _____ : 4

   (c) 5 : 8 = 20 : _____      (d) 24 : 6 = _____ : 3

   (e) 9 : 10 = _____ : 40     (f) 2 : _____ = 8 : 16

   (g) 4 : 5 = _____ : 35      (h) 30 : _____ = 6 : 3

   (i) 9 : 3 = 3 : _____       (j) _____ : 5 = 5 : 25

   (k) 10 : 4 = 5 : _____      (l) _____ : 3 = 24 : 18

4. The length of a rectangle is 60 in. and its width is 48 in. Find the ratio of the length to the width.

5. A ribbon 40 cm long is cut into two pieces. One piece is 16 cm long. Find the ratio of the length of the longer piece to the length of the shorter piece.

6. Peter saves $52. Sumin saves $20 more than Peter. Find the ratio of Peter's savings to Sumin's savings.

# EXERCISE 3

1.  The ratio of the number of apples to the number of oranges is 7 : 4. There are 60 oranges. How many apples are there?

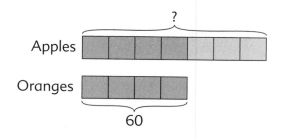

2.  Sulin cuts a ribbon into two pieces in the ratio 5 : 3. The shorter piece is 42 cm long. What is the length of the original ribbion?

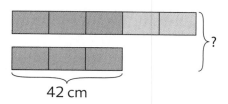

3. The ratio of the cost of a skirt to the cost of a blouse is 8 : 5. If the skirt costs $24 more than the blouse, find the cost of the blouse.

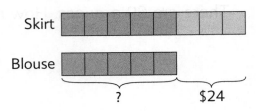

Skirt

Blouse

? $24

---

4. John and Peter shared $280 in the ratio 7 : 3. How much more money did John receive than Peter?

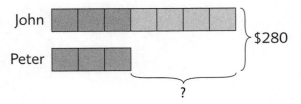

John

Peter

$280

?

# EXERCISE 4

1.

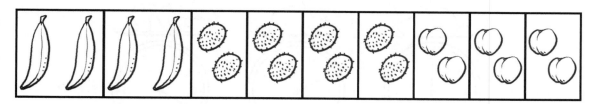

The ratio of the number of bananas to the number of kiwis to the

number of apricots is _____ : _____ : _____.

---

2.

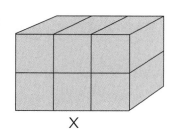

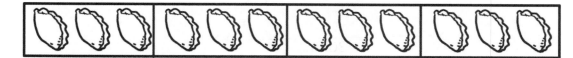

The ratio of the number of cupcakes to the number of chicken wings

to the number of pastries is _____ : _____ : _____.

---

3.

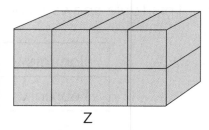

The ratio of the volume of Solid X to the volume of Solid Y to the

volume of Solid Z is _____ : _____ : _____.

4.

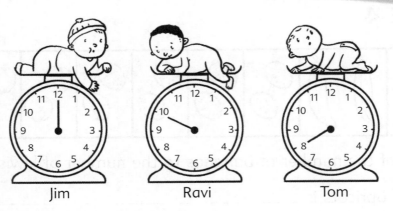

Jim's weight : Ravi's weight : Tom's weight

= _____ : _____ : _____

5.

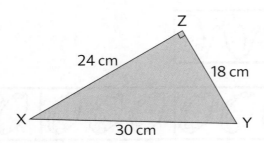

Length of XZ : Length of YZ : Length of XY

= _____ : _____ : _____

6.  This table shows Mingli's savings for 3 months.

| January | $12 |
| --- | --- |
| February | $12 |
| March | $8 |

Savings in January : Savings in February : Savings in March

= _____ : _____ : _____

# EXERCISE 5

1.  A box contains blue, green and white beads. The ratio of the number
    of blue beads to the number of green beads to the number of white
    beads is 5 : 2 : 3. If there are 90 blue beads, how many beads are
    there altogether?

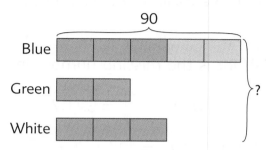

2.  A piece of wire 45 cm long is bent to form a triangle. If the sides of
    the triangle are in the ratio 3 : 2 : 4, find the length of the longest
    side.

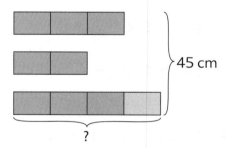

# REVIEW 6

1. Write the following in figures.

   (a) three hundred sixty-eight thousand, seven hundred six

   (b) five million twenty-one thousand

2. What is the missing number in each ?

   (a) $56{,}074 - \boxed{\phantom{0}} = 52{,}074$

   (b) $16 \times 125 = 125 \times 2 \times \boxed{\phantom{0}}$

   (c) $28 \times 25 = 100 \times \boxed{\phantom{0}}$

   (d) $999 + 998 = 2000 - \boxed{\phantom{0}}$

3. What is the **smallest** whole number that can be placed in each 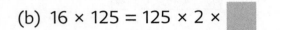?

   (a) $35 + \boxed{\phantom{0}} > 60$

   (b) $\boxed{\phantom{0}} - 28 > 79$

   (c) $106 < \boxed{\phantom{0}} \times 8$

   (d) $5 < \boxed{\phantom{0}} \div 4$

4. What is the **greatest** whole number that can be placed in each ?

   (a) $100 + \boxed{\phantom{0}} < 300$

   (b) $\boxed{\phantom{0}} - 2 < 20$

   (c) $\boxed{\phantom{0}} \times 7 < 100$

   (d) $8 > \boxed{\phantom{0}} \div 6$

5. Find the prime factorization of 72.

<br>

6. Find the value of the following expressions.

   (a) $7 \times 5 \times 8$

   (b) $96 \div 3 \div 4$

   (c) $12 \times (10 - 5)$

   (d) $70 + 24 \div 6 - 4$

   (e) $(32 + 8 + 30) \times 2$

   (f) $63 \div 9 + 20 \div 10$

7. $\frac{2}{3}$ of a jug of water is 6 cups. Find the total number of cups of water in the jug.

8. Divide in compound units.

   (a) 3 yd 1 ft $\div$ 2 = [ ] yd [ ] ft

   (b) 2 lb 10 oz $\div$ 6 = [ ] lb [ ] oz

   (c) 6 gal 3 qt $\div$ 3 = [ ] gal [ ] qt

   (d) 2 ft 8 in. $\div$ 4 = [ ] ft [ ] in.

9. Find the value of the following.

   (a) $\frac{1}{3}$ of 24 yd

   (b) $\frac{4}{5}$ of 35 in.

   (c) $1\frac{1}{2}$ of 14 oz

   (d) $\frac{5}{6}$ of 12 gal

10. The rectangle is made up of 6 unit squares. If the area of the rectangle is 54 cm², find its perimeter.

11. The perimeter of a square is 32 m.

    (a) Find the length of one side of the square.

    (b) Find its area.

12. The perimeter of a rectangle is 32 cm. If its width is 6 cm, find its length and area.

    6 cm

    ?

13. The area of the shaded part is $\frac{1}{3}$ of the area of the rectangle. Find the area of the rectangle.

    18 m

    16 m

14. The length and the width of a rectangle are in the ratio 5 : 3. The length of the rectangle is 20 in.

    (a) Find its width.

    (b) Find its area.

    (c) Find its perimeter.

15. The sides of a triangle are in the ratio 5 : 2 : 4.
    The longest side of the triangle is 15 cm.

    (a) Find its shortest side.

    (b) Find its perimeter.

16. The ratio of Gary's weight to Andy's weight is 4 : 5.
    Their total weight is 117 kg.

    (a) Find Andy's weight.

    (b) Find Gary's weight.

17. The ratio of the height of a tree to the length of its
    shadow is 3 : 2. The height of the tree is 15 m.
    Find the length of its shadow.

18. Find the perimeter and area of each figure.
    (All the lines meet at right angles.)
    (a)                                    (b)

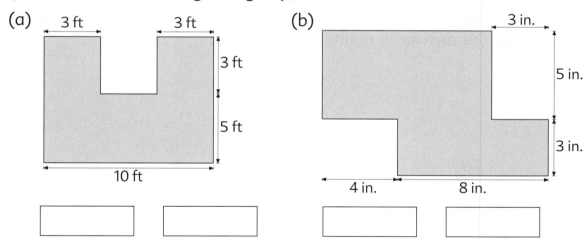

19. A rectangular prism measures 12 ft long, 6 ft wide
    and 7 ft high. Find its surface area.

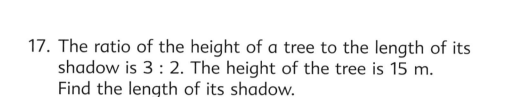

20. The ratio of Bill's money to Henry's money was 5 : 6. After Bill spent $800 on a TV set, the ratio became 1 : 2. How much money did Bill have at first?

---

21. A basket weighs 12 oz. A watermelon weighing 7 lb 9 oz is added to the basket. What is the total weight of the basket and watermelon? (Give the answer in pounds and ounces.)

22. The total weight of Morgan, Emily and Ashley is 243 lb. Morgan is 30 lb heavier than Emily. Emily is 6 lb lighter than Ashley. What is Ashley's weight?

Blank